Enhancing Learning through Technology in Lifelong Learning

Fresh ideas, innovative strategies

25 creative tools for using technology in your practice

Steve Ingle and Vicky Duckworth

 Open University Press

Open University Press
McGraw-Hill Education
McGraw-Hill House
Shoppenhangers Road
Maidenhead
Berkshire
England
SL6 2QL

email: enquiries@openup.co.uk
world wide web: www.openup.co.uk

and Two Penn Plaza, New York, NY 10121-2289, USA

First published 2013

A catalogue record of this book is available from the British Library

ISBN10: 0-33-524640-0 (pb)
ISBN13: 978-0-33-524640-3 (pb)
eISBN: 978-0-33-524641-0

Library of Congress Cataloging-in-Publication Data
CIP data has been applied for

Typeset by Aptara Inc., India
Printed and bound by CPI Group (UK) Ltd, Croydon, CR0 4YY

Enhancing Learning through Technology in Lifelong Learning

Fresh ideas, innovative strategies

Steve would like to dedicate this book to Grandma 'Joy' and Marjorie Hughes; two inspirational and selfless individuals.

Vicky would like to dedicate this book to Nana Johanna Kippax (nee Duckworth) and her childhood mate, Jane Vernon, still missed.

Praise for this book

"This welcome book fills a real need within lifelong learning literature, through providing an exploration of the different ICT technologies available to students and teachers in the sector that combines the practical and applicable with the theoretical and reflective. Through the course of this book, the authors introduce and analyse a number of key theoretical themes, such as digital wisdom and digital literacy, providing an accessible entry point to rich and complex ideas. They also provide the reader with a considerable number of helpful summaries of readily available technologies that cover relevant topics such as presentations and e-portfolios, linking them to a critical understanding of pedagogy and inclusion. Throughout, the authors maintain a writing style that is always engaging and easy to follow, reinforced by practitioners' case studies that demonstrate how e-learning can move from being the property of the technological fetishist to an aspect of the professional practice of all teachers in the lifelong learning sector. I cannot think of another book on this subject that has managed to accomplish this."

Dr Jonathan Tummons, Teesside University, UK

"This book is an indispensable guide to the discovery and use of learning technologies for new and experienced teachers in the lifelong learning sector.

The structure and presentation make it easy to navigate and a pleasure to read. There is a very useful overview of relevant learning theory and discussion of key issues relating to developments in technology. The heart of the book provides concise and accessible introductions to twenty-five learning technologies with ideas about integrating them into learning and teaching.

This isn't just a book about technology; it is, more importantly, a book about learning."

Peter Scales, University of Derby, UK

"This book is addressed to practitioners in search of "digital wisdom" and I was immediately inspired to explore the activities with my students. It offers accessible but non-patronising information, definitions and terminology related to specific applications and tools. These are packaged in short 2-3 page sections that are easy to read and include practical tips and online links to the applications. Reflection points are built in throughout and each section includes an example of how the tool has been used by a classroom practitioner.

The authors address their readers as creative practitioners who are, as a matter of course, looking for better, more exciting ways to learn and teach. The positive tone and clear writing de-mystifies the whole idea of using digital tools for learning and makes such explorations sound fun, easy and inevitable.

Although the main idea is to offer quick access to techniques for classroom use these are put into context by a clear introduction that explains basic concepts of approaches to learning with technology and by a narrative running throughout that "connects the dots" of the specific applications.

There is surely something here for everyone, no matter what the level of their existing expertise."

Mary Hamilton, Lancaster University, UK

Contents

Acknowledgements

The authors wish to extend their most grateful thanks to all those who have contributed their time, ideas and inspiration in shaping this text for the benefit of other practitioners.

In particular, thanks go to Claire Sutton, Pat Link, Simon Williams, Louise Lostyn, Naomi Wilson, Mark Lane, Jo Riley, Bekah Funnings, Beckie Knight and all current practitioners who have illustrated their innovative use of learning technologies:

Dawne Bell – Edge Hill University
Jonathan Bishop – Nelson and Colne College
Samantha Jane Catterall – Bury College
Claire Elliott – Penwortham Girls' High School
Alan Goodenough – Blackburn College
Peter Grist – The Manchester College
Dan Hodge – Kendal College
Karen McCormack – Edge Hill University
Kim Murden – Worden Sports College
Adam Palin – Manchester Metropolitan University
John Picken – Blackburn College University Centre
Lucy Stone – Amateur Swimming Association
Martin Troughton – Kendal College
David Wooff – Edge Hill University

We would like to thank the following for their friendship and intellectual stimulation:

Mary Hamilton, Jonathan Tummons, Yvon Appleby, Angela Brzeski, Jill Cochane, Janet Lord and Sue Watmore.

About this book

This book provides a source of ideas, case studies and links on how to use new and emerging technologies in innovative and creative ways in the classroom, lecture hall, workshop, salon and studio in your subject specialism – ideas and tools that apply to a diverse range of subjects which may span from A level literature, to construction, to hairdressing.

We recognize the diversity of the sector and the learners, and have identified key themes to promote effective teaching and learning:

- I want to find new ways to keep my learners engaged, to keep them on task and to motivate them to attend their classes.
- I know that outstanding teachers often take a risk in their approach to teaching and learning. I want to try something new to develop my own practice.
- I want to offer more personalized learning opportunities for my students. This can be difficult in a large class with only one tutor.
- I want to support my least able learners and stretch and challenge my most able learners.
- I want to learn new skills to develop as a new professional practitioner.
- I want to demonstrate that I can meet the expected professional standards of teachers, tutors and trainers.

Whatever your rationale for developing and enhancing your practice, this text provides an accessible, practical and overall essential guide for practitioners who place learning and learners at the heart of their practice. This book is aimed specifically at practitioners working in the lifelong learning sector, including those teaching learners aged 14 plus in schools and colleges, those teaching adults in community learning venues and those working with undergraduate and postgraduate students in further and higher education institutions.

We use the terms 'practitioner' and 'tutor' interchangeably to indicate anyone working across this diverse sector – for example, teachers, tutors, trainers, lecturers, support workers, managers and administrators. As well as new and more experienced practitioners, we hope this book will prove useful for teachers in training looking to expand their developing knowledge and skills and to take the risks so often necessary to deliver truly outstanding and engaging teaching and learning.

We recognize that those working across the sector face increasing pressures in demonstrating purposeful engagement with technology, providing outstanding teaching and learning and striving for best value in an age of funding cuts, mergers and incomparable change. Professional standards for those working in schools, universities and the lifelong learning sector reinforce the requirement for today's professional tutors to utilize new and emerging technology appropriately, where it has the potential to enhance the learning experience. Internal audits, external observations by the Inspectorate, peer assessment and changing learner expectations are all drivers for practitioners to ensure they are confident and skilled to:

- use a range of effective and appropriate teaching and learning techniques to engage and motivate independent learners
- select, develop and implement a range of effective resources and assessment tools which make appropriate use of new and emerging technologies.

Learner experiences with new and emerging technologies should take place in an environment where technology is important and enjoyable. The activities should be personally meaningful, and learners should have these powerful experiences as often as possible. However, the prevalence of technology brought into the classroom can be a real challenge for practitioners and tutors who do not use technology or cannot model the appropriate use for technology in a classroom. We hope that, as busy professionals, readers will find this essential guide invaluable as a source of fresh ideas and innovative strategies to engage and retain learners through the use of emerging technologies.

Chapter 1 presents the theoretical voice and a rationale for the use of technology in today's twenty-first century learning environment, as practitioners prepare themselves for the arrival of technologically mature twenty-first century learners with high expectations of their learning journey. Theoretical, philosophical and practical debates on the digital divide are unpacked and discussed, with prompts for personal reflections on how these debates may impact on your own professional practice, skills development and action planning. An alternative model of reflection is proposed, to guide and empower practitioners through following the flow of reflective practice, in order to effectively embrace the significant and rapid changes affecting both the educational landscape and the technological horizon.

Part Two then presents 25 practical ideas for the use of a range of accessible, intuitive and financially viable technological tools. Busy practitioners need tools which do not take days of training, or substantial departmental budgets, to acquire and use. Many tutors lack confidence in the use of technical equipment, or avoid harnessing the benefits of technology in their learning environments due to competing time pressures or concerns over skills and competence. The range of tools has been selected to offer something for everyone, from the competent early adopter to the experienced practitioner looking for ideas to integrate technology into their lesson tomorrow morning.

Tools are presented in a user-friendly and accessible format, offering key ideas and practical activities which ground new and emerging technologies in real practice through the use of case studies and reflection points. Whatever the level of technical ability, we are confident that teaching practitioners, teachers in training and those supporting learning will all find new ideas to enhance their approaches to creative teaching and learning with the use of technology.

In the final chapter we explore the application of technology in practice and illustrate how two mature students have embraced technology throughout their learning journeys. This provides a rich narrative of how lecturers experience technology in their own learning as well as with their learners, and they offer advice for practitioners of a digital, knowledge age.

PART ONE
Introduction

Introduction

A day in the life of Sam...

Battery 100%. The alarm goes off on my mobile. It's 7.30 a.m. and I really need to get up and ready for college. I've just got time to check out the updates on Facebook; what went on last night and with whom?!

Battery 92%. The bus journey can be a drag. With traffic, it can take almost an hour to travel the 12 miles into college. I send a text to my friend to tell him I might be late – again. I check the news via the BBC app on my smartphone, take my turn in the online Scrabble game and access my college timetable via the mobile VLE page. Today is a busy day.

Battery 77%. I sign in to the college Wi-Fi network; this speeds things up. Time to go over last night's homework task for media studies on genre. I spoke my film review into this great new speech-to-text app on my phone and emailed the converted text to my Gmail account. Now what did I say? Mr Malik is bound to ask me to read it out in class today.

Battery 59%. Over lunch I respond to a few text messages, update my Facebook status and re-tweet a post about yesterday's football result. I use the terminal in the canteen to log into the college ePortfolio and check the results of my last exam – Distinction! Although my attendance is only showing 85 per cent; I need to get my last medical appointment changed to authorized absence. I send an instant message to Student Services.

Battery 42%. I take a picture of the whiteboard in Mrs Knight's class. Her notes are always so useful and it saves me time copying every word down, which seems to take me much longer than everyone else. She tells us about a really useful revision website. I add it to my favourites list to explore later.

Battery 31%. Six people 'like' my last Facebook status; it was funny. I've been tagged in some embarrassing photos from Saturday's party; I hope Auntie Jean doesn't see them. The bus is caught in traffic again. I bring up the whiteboard photo from this afternoon's English class and go over the main points again. I wish I'd recorded what she was saying.

Battery 22%. Sooooo funny. The YouTube clip my friend sent me had me in stitches. After dinner I tweet a link *#OMGcat.* I also watch a revision clip on genre made by last year's students. Mr Malik wants us to work in groups to create our own videos this year. I want ours to get top marks (and to be funny).

Battery 14%. A long day. Looking forward to going on study leave next month. I check my timetable online for tomorrow. Mrs Knight has sent us an email with a link to a new online book-marking list she has set up for Unit 2 – I will look at some of those tomorrow on the bus. Hope I'm not late again. Alarm set, phone back on charge...

Sam – A level student in a sixth form college

Sam's account is typical of how many of today's learners use and apply technology as a seamless integration to both their living (social) and learning lives (public and private). Technology for many learners in a digital, knowledge age is not an *extra* or a *bolt-on* but a natural augmentation (expansion) to their lived experiences in the public and private domains of their life – for example, private: in the home; public: at school, college, university and the workplace.

For Sam, then, the digital tools at her fingertips allow her to easily and effectively converse, collaborate and capture. She has developed the skills and language to operate and communicate in a digital landscape: an online world of downloads, wireless connections (Wi-Fi), applications (apps), social networking and multimedia. Her tutors, Mrs Knight and Mr Malik, did not grow up in the digital world of today. For them, the cassette tape, personal stereo and colour television were the pioneering technological developments of their formative years. They have seen many changes in their professional careers, both to the popular educational policy initiatives of the day and to the use of emerging technologies applied to practice. They are aware of some of the general pedagogical benefits that technology can bring to learning, such as more 'SPACE':

- Sharing
- Personalization
- Accessibility
- Communication
- Engagement.

They have read case studies of practice exploring the tangible benefits of e-learning (see JISC 2008, 2012), which illustrate the impact of technology on exam results, student satisfaction, retention and social equality. They have also investigated rigorous research reports which identify the positive impact that technology in learning can have on student achievement levels and outcomes (Tamim et al. 2011).

 **Find out more**

The JISC Learning and Teaching Committee presents a diverse range of 37 detailed online case studies which explore evidence that technology-enhanced learning is delivering tangible benefits for learners, teachers and institutions.

Click: www.jiscinfonet.ac.uk/case-studies/tangible

Tamim et al. (2011) are aware of how pervasive technology is becoming in the physical and online learning environments, both from learners' ownership and use of their own devices, and the investment in technology hardware and software by their institutions. They have begun to explore accessible ways of integrating consumer technologies they are comfortable and familiar with from their personal lives, such as email, websites and video, but feel they would like to know more about other technologies which may potentially have a positive impact on students' experience, their learning and ultimately achievement.

Reflection point

- As a practitioner, how do you view technology and its role in our living, working and learning lives?
- How can you harness the benefits of technology to enhance learning, and where do we find the tools we can easily embed into our practice?

This book is structured into discrete parts to provide an essential resource for both new and beginning, and more experienced, tutors and practitioners. It is designed to illuminate and explore some of these questions, providing very practical advice for those looking to develop their use of technology in their approach to teaching, learning and assessment, whether in a physical or online learning environment.

After this introduction, Chapter 1 provides a theoretical voice and the background to the use of new and emerging technologies in lifelong learning. It encourages practitioners to reflect on the changing context of the lifelong learning sector and the implications for their own practice and development. We explore some of the current debates around the use of information and communications technology (ICT) in education, providing an overview of some of the theoretical, philosophical and practical considerations for those looking to start using, or expand their use of, technology to enhance and mediate learning.

We explore the debate around the needs of twenty-first century learners, the so-called 'network generation'. As these young people travel through the compulsory education sector, what needs and expectations regarding the use of technology in lessons will they have and demand when they reach the college classroom? The notions of the 'digital learner' are unpacked and explored, with useful prompts for reflection on existing and future practice. Are the tried and tested pedagogical approaches of yesterday still compatible with the learners of today? How do new millennium learners view the use of technology in both their living and learning lives – and what implications does this have for us as teachers, lecturers and trainers in the current educational climate?

We explore 'digital divides' between learners and many tutors, and place this against the backdrop of concerns relating to the use of technology and the developing learning preferences and behaviours of the 'new millennium learners', for example the impact on standards of written literacy, plagiarism issues, shortening attention spans and the need for constant stimulation.

Now, in the twenty-first century, new and emerging technologies are appearing every day for tutors to think about. Learners arrive at school, college, university or their training workplace with the latest mobile device. Learning environments (both physical and online) are updated with new equipment, features and functions. There is great pressure for practitioners to embrace these changes and demonstrate engagement.

So what impact does this have on learners?

With the advent of technology across all fields of learning, the ways in which learners store and retrieve information for further use has dramatically changed. As such, multimedia, interactive technologies and new ways of developing collaboration are approaches which can be successfully utilized for learning. Chapter 1 highlights the call by some for a new approach to teaching and theories of learning for a knowledge age.

New technologies can be employed in a creative way. The willingness and confidence of the tutor to explore, model and experiment with new pedagogic approaches may be viewed as critical to developing the effective use of technologies for teaching and learning.

Tutors have a professional responsibility to learn more about what they teach (including the updating of their subject specialism) and how they teach it (developing new techniques), which includes using technology in meaningful and innovative ways. Whether new or more experienced professionals, we need to continually pause, evaluate and consider how the changing landscape of policy and practice may impact on our work.

We are in a time of significant and rapid change, both in terms of educational and institutional policy and practice, coupled with the dynamic shifts in technological advancement. Together, their associated impact on learners, learning, infrastructure, society and culture cannot be underestimated. Finding time for quality and meaningful reflection on our existing practice can empower us to react, respond and be empowered by change, to ensure we continue to thrive as effective educationalists who meet the diverse needs of all our learners.

Chapter 1 presents an alternative model to guide the flow of reflective practice. The 'IRIS' lens of reflection encourages a solutions-based approach to addressing barriers or concerns to professional practice. Four sequential lenses are presented to guide users to consider how their existing strengths and ongoing skills development can be used to identify potential interventions. The model encourages practitioners to flow through the four stages of reflection, focusing on how interventions may be implemented practically and what impact they may have on both learning and future practice.

Finally, Chapter 1 briefly considers the issues around the speed of technological development and how practitioners and tutors can stay up to date with emerging tools and techniques. There is a discussion around the use of learners' own technology and their own expertise, and how this can be a positive resource for those finding it difficult to keep up with constant change. The chapter concludes with a look to the future.

Part Two of this book provides a wide range of very practical ideas and suggestions for those looking to expand their 'tutor's toolkit' through the use of technology-enhanced learning. Twenty-five tools are introduced, illustrated and supported by practical and accessible ways in which they might be used in the classroom, lecture hall, seminar room, salon, workshop or online learning environment:

- links to pedagogic practice
- links to popular websites and online tools

- ideas for developing subject-specific content
- development and extension ideas
- reflective tasks
- case studies
- further reading
- hints and tips on staying safe and secure.

We also hear the practitioner's voice in this chapter, with a range of examples showing how practitioners are using these tools in their approach to teaching, learning and assessment to enhance learning, save time, promote active and collaborative learning, and enhance the progress and outcomes of their learners.

We invite you to 'give it a go', with links to online tools and resources to experiment and practise yourself. We have actively tried to avoid impressive but expensive commercial products and, with significant pressures on budgets, those options which are free or of very low cost to educators have been prioritized. There are few things more disheartening than investing valuable time in learning a new piece of software, integrating it into your scheme of work and curriculum plan, introducing it to your learners, and subsequently finding that the licence has been discontinued as the financial burden is unsustainable!

Each tool has been selected for its easy access and intuitive design. If it takes more than a few minutes to grasp the basics and see some results, then it is unlikely to be adopted into mainstream practice by the majority. Whichever sphere of the lifelong learning sector you work in, time is precious. Preparing sessions, taking classes, attending meetings, completing paperwork, complying with audits, participating in training, marking assessments, problem solving, troubleshooting, resolving conflict are – to name but a few – the regular duties of the schoolteacher, the college lecturer and the professional trainer. To be really useful in your approach, technology should be intuitive, easy to use, time saving and improve outcomes.

There will always be the 'early adopters', the technically able who are the first to explore and experiment with the very latest devices and software. But there are also the 'digital tourists', those who approach the use of technology in their teaching with some trepidation, some scepticism, perhaps even some fear. Whichever end of the spectrum you identify with, the range of tools presented in Part Two of this book should offer something that everyone can easily integrate into their practice, in an appropriate and useful way.

The focus is very much on how each technological tool may have the power to enhance learning. We take a 'learning first, technology second' mantra. Technology has the power to entertain, engage, inspire and connect, but also to distract. It can take up large amounts of preparatory and teaching time and so its use must be carefully considered. We encourage all practitioners to carefully explore how each tool presented could enhance the outcomes for learners, from promoting engagement to maximizing achievement, but also to consider some of the potential barriers to use that may hinder or discourage you from adopting them into your practice, such as e-safety, reliability and accessibility. By considering issues now, we can work to reduce and remove barriers for the significant benefits to both learner and practitioner.

Having explored some of the academic and philosophical debates around the use of technology and listened to the experiences of practitioners applying technology in their practice, the final chapter in the book highlights the learners' voice and their experiences of how technology has impacted and influenced their own learning journeys.

We hear from Claire, a mature student of adult nursing, and her personal journey from school to university. She offers a personal insight into her own use of technologies in her learning and offers advice for practitioners seeking to use technologies appropriately to engage and motivate learners.

We also hear from Pat, a trainee secondary schoolteacher, and his experiences of technology and how it has facilitated his learning and helped him overcome barriers to learning after being diagnosed with dyslexia.

Chapter 1 Teaching in a digital, knowledge age

In Chapter 1 we present a brief overview of the ongoing debate around technology and pedagogy and some of the considerations that arise for your own professional practice as a practitioner in the digital, knowledge age. We explore a range of themes which propose timely considerations and reflection points for those re-examining their approaches to teaching, learning and assessment in the twenty-first century.

By the end of this chapter, you will have considered the following questions:

- Who are the learners of the digital, knowledge age, and do they really learn 'differently'?
- What can twenty-first-century practitioners do to respond effectively to these changes?
- How can the power of emerging technologies be harnessed for pedagogic gain and positive impact?
- How can we 'reflect for action' to overcome barriers and concerns about change and the use of technology to support and enhance learning?

Introduction

Do you have a hashtag? What's your Skype name? Can you scan a QR code? When was the last time you took a stroll through Second Life? Have you ever sent an IM? If these questions seem incomprehensible, does it really matter? The new language of the digital, knowledge age may seem confusing and challenging, but if this is increasingly the adopted discourse of our learners, do we as practitioners have a duty to learn the language, and associated knowledge and skills, in order to continue to contribute effectively to the teaching and learning conversation?

Whether you are a tutor or practitioner in a school, college, university, community venue, prison or work-based provider, the ubiquity of technology in our own lives and the lives of our learners is undeniable. Learning environments have also seen change and continue to evolve in their design and function. Whether teaching in classrooms, lecture theatres, workshops, kitchens or salons, many have seen the impact of technology on their facilities. Blackboards have become white, and now interactive. Chalk gave way to the marker and now the e-pen. Textbooks are increasingly presented as e-books; notepads are for typing on, not writing in. Homework and assignments are increasingly emailed or submitted to the virtual learning environment (VLE), not handed in.

Whether you love it or loathe it, the focus on technology for learning is becoming an ever louder voice in the conversation on pedagogy and educational practice. Driven by social and technological changes, it is clear that economic implications are also having a significant impact on sharpening the focus for finding technological solutions to a leaner and more cost-effective educational landscape. Larger class sizes, smaller budgets, learners as consumers, finding more effective ways of learning, and the true globalization of education are all contributory factors to the ongoing dialogue on the impact of technology-mediated learning.

When we consider globalization and its effects on education we might identify an age of democracy, freedom of thought, ideas and acquired knowledge that allows learners (and us) to think globally rather than locally and nationally. With the rapid and seemingly constant development of new and emerging technologies, there has also been a change of concepts around space and time. Consider the speed and the wealth of access to global information now available at the touch of a button or the swipe of a mobile screen. These developments change the boundaries of what knowledge is and how it is shaped. Computers in schools, colleges and universities are not a new phenomenon; they have been used in classrooms in increasingly larger numbers for the last two decades. However, their presence has been slow to translate into substantially changed practice or widespread use except in relatively straightforward applications such as the approaches you probably use in your day-to-day work as a practitioner: sending emails, word processing and using presentation software.

Unpacking the digital divide: are we talking the same language?

I use some technology in both my home and professional life; I send text messages and emails, create PowerPoint presentations and keep in touch with friends via Facebook. I've been teaching for a while now and I have certainly seen some changes, not only to my role and at college but also in the learners themselves. They seem to be online all the time, constantly checking their mobile phones and updating their online 'status'. It's difficult to enforce the college rule on mobiles in class.

My students use acronyms and terminology I've never heard before – it's like a different language. They seem to think that a quick Google search will give them all the answers to their assignments. I'm concerned that I'm getting left behind. Some of my colleagues are using technology in exciting ways in their sessions – the learners tell me. I've been told that we are going to be moving to online learning much more. But does all this technology really make that much of a difference? My job is to get them through their assignments, not to entertain!

Linda – lecturer in a further education college

The comments made by Linda may feel familiar. As tutors, it often seems that we have been operating in a period of continual change, both in terms of educational policy and practice and in the way rapid technological developments are shaping the lives and practices of our learners and ourselves. While we focus on ensuring we are compliant with the latest national and institutional interventions, it is also important to ensure we keep abreast of the changing technological landscape, its impact on the way our learners live and learn, and the way we shape and develop our professional practice.

Back in 2001, American writer and speaker Mark Prensky issued an arguably controversial challenge to educators, which prompted a lively, lengthy and ongoing debate on the implications of a potential divide between learners and their tutors: 'the single biggest problem facing education today is that our digital immigrant instructors, who speak an outdated language (that of the pre-digital age), are struggling to teach a population that speaks an entirely new language.' (Prensky 2001)

Popularizing the 'digital native' and 'digital immigrant' debate, the metaphor highlights the cultural divide between young people's ease and comfort with technology, which has surrounded, immersed and shaped their developing lives, and the more deliberate ways in which many tutors consider, explore, reject or develop the use of technology in their lives and professional practice. It is argued that digital natives are those who represent generations who have grown up with the 'new' technology of the internet, email, video games, digital music, mobile phones and all the other tools of the digital age. Other descriptions for today's learners, who have been raised in a digital world – generally accepted in the literature as post-1980 – include:

- IM (instant-message) Generation (Lenhart et al. 2001)
- Homo Zappiens (Veen 2003)
- Cyberkids (Holloway and Valentine 2003)
- Net Generation (Net Gen) (Tapscott 1998, 2008)
- Gen-Xers (Oblinger 2003)
- Millennials (Howe and Strauss 2000)
- the Gamer Generation (Carstens and Beck 2005)
- New Millennium Learners (Pedro 2006)
- Social Cyborgs (Campbell and Finegan 2011).

Whatever the label, twenty-first-century learners have often been characterized as a group definable by their particular learning preferences and behaviours, shaped by their growth in a digital age, including:

- fluency in multiple media use
- active learning based on experience
- an ability to multitask and deal simultaneously with difference sources of digital information (for example, instant messages, text messages, internet pages and digital media)
- use of social networking and collaborative media and so-called Web 2.0 technologies and applications
- a non-linear approach to accessing and using information sources and navigating resources
- constant and instant online communication and connectivity
- sharing information culture.

(See Tapscott 1998; Prensky 2001; Veen 2003; Oblinger 2004; Dede 2005; Thomas 2011.)

Reflection point

- What is your experience of twenty-first-century learners?
- Do you feel that the learning approaches and preferences of students have changed?
- How would you describe these changes – what have you noticed?

When I go home to visit my parents, I see my younger sister and the way she deals with information and technology. She is often found at the computer communicating with over a dozen friends simultaneously through online instant messaging. At the same time, she is sending a text message, listening to music and uploading photos from her iPad to Facebook. She tells me that she is not doing well at school, but I see so many complex and transferable skills that are so valuable in a digital age.

Paul – trainee secondary maths teacher

If you are working in a high school or further education college environment, you may have noticed some traits in the behaviours and preferences of your own learners similar to those identified by Paul, but do the learners of a whole network generation really learn in a different way? As a result of growing up in this digital age and being immersed in the use of technology in many aspects of their daily lives, Prensky (2001, 2011) argues that today's students 'think and process information fundamentally differently from their predecessors' and are native speakers of the 'digital age language'. It is argued that tutors, as digital immigrants, or newcomers, may well begin to embrace and support the use of technologies in their own approaches to teaching, learning and assessment but this may not always be aligned with the way our digitally native students approach their learning – they will still speak with an 'accent'!

Palfrey and Gasser (2008) extend Prensky's distinction further with the suggestion of a third group they call the 'digital settler', defined as those born well before the Net Gen, but who have adopted new technologies from the beginning. These learners may be more mature but are also comfortable with their adoption and use of technologies in their social and learning lives. Those working with older learners in various aspects of the lifelong learning sector may be able to identify settlers and the technological skills they bring to the learning environment. The adult and community learning classroom may well include a wide range of ages, abilities and levels of comfort with technology as natives, immigrants and settlers mix together in one learning environment.

Reflection point

- How do you identify yourself against the backdrop of the digital native, newcomer, tourist, immigrant and settler debate?
- Do you feel that age plays a crucial factor in the way learners approach technology, the skills they have and the way they perceive technology – as an extension of themselves or as a very separate function?

Researchers have also identified divisions in the use, capabilities and *perceptions* of technology between students and their tutors (see Oblinger 2003; Conole et al. 2006; Hughes 2009). The contrast in comfort with technology means that many students can find the use of technology in education to be disappointing, often considering themselves more internet-savvy than their tutors. For some practitioners, this can highlight a difficult tension; the tutor is supposed to be the more knowledgeable expert, the one to guide and inform, to teach. To acknowledge that our learners may be more skilled and technologically aware can be viewed as a challenge to the positioning of power and control in the traditional roles of teacher and student.

The level of capability and skill as a factor influencing comfort levels also acknowledges the importance of professional development for educators and its impact on addressing barriers to technology adoption and experimentation. If practitioners, as digital newcomers or immigrants, do not have access to appropriate training and skills development opportunities, is it reasonable to assume that their approach to teaching and learning will embrace some of the technologies that many natives may see as a natural part of their lives? On a national level, the resourcing and prioritization of practitioner ICT skills development has seen a process of debate, review and reform. Following the 2010 post-election spending review, the abolishment of British Educational Communications and Technology Agency (BECTA) (the UK government agency which promoted technology in schools) in 2011 sent a clear signal to some about the commitment to ongoing staff development and skills enhancement of twenty-first-century teachers and lecturers. Table 1.1 shows current alternative sources of support for developing the ICT skills of teaching practitioners.

Reflection point

- Do you feel that you have the knowledge and skills to embrace technology effectively in your approach to teaching and learning?
- Have professional development opportunities effectively addressed any barriers to technology adoption for you?
- Have you identified any areas where additional skills development would be useful in facilitating your use of learning technologies?
- How do you feel about acknowledging your level of digital competence to your own learners?
- Are you happy to encourage technology-savvy learners to take the lead when demonstrating how to use equipment or online services?

In an investigation into the use of technology by New Millennium Learners (NML), Pedro (2006) suggests that attitudes and expectations regarding learning and teaching have evolved radically from previous generations, and while teachers were once in command of the opportunities to use e-learning innovations in education situations, the increased use of technology by learners in their personal and private lives means that their ICT skills are outperforming those of their tutors.

Accordingly, Pedro suggests that students' expectations around the opportunities for collaborative working and networking, the degree of learning personalization and the standards of digital quality could have changed dramatically and be completely different from the ones held by their teachers. This could lead to a growing gap between student and teacher perceptions of the quality of the educational experience, or even lead to some students becoming increasingly disaffected.

So what does this mean to you as a practitioner?

This perspective raises some important questions. If students feel that their learning experience does not meet their expectations, this may have significant implications for retention, achievement, and ultimately

Table 1.1 Sources of national support for ICT skills development of teaching practitioners

Association for Learning Technology (ALT)	www.alt.ac.uk	ALT is a membership organization in the learning technology field, with the aim of ensuring that use of learning technology is effective and efficient, informed by research and practice, and grounded in an understanding of the underlying technologies, their capabilities and the situations into which they are placed. ALT provides a range of publications, events, conferences and discussion groups, as well as a peer-based certification scheme for learning technologists.
The Association for Information Technology in Teacher Education (ITTE)	www.itte.org.uk	ITTE is a membership organization that aims to further the integration of information technologies in teacher education. Members have access to a range of publications including the *Technology, Pedagogy and Education* journal, a national conference and networking opportunities.
Futurelab	www.futurelab.org.uk	Futurelab is an independent organization which aims to promote and develop creative and innovative approaches to education, teaching and learning. Futurelab's work focuses on curriculum innovation, digital literacy and participation, learning spaces, play and computer games, and assessment. It offers practitioners a range of teaching resources, research-informed publications, professional development workshops and events and networking opportunities.
The ICT association (Naace)	www.naace.co.uk	Formerly the National Association of Advisers for Computers in Education, Naace is a professional association representing educational technology in the schools sector. Naace supports practitioners through networking opportunities, peer support, resources, events and training, including practitioner accreditation in ICT continuing professional development (CPD).
JISC	www.jisc.ac.uk	JISC (formerly the Joint Information Systems Committee) is a large organization funded by the UK post-16 and higher education funding bodies as well as the Research Councils. JISC supports further and higher education institutions to develop the effective use of digital technologies through resources, knowledge and expertise. JISC funds a wide range of national shared services, providing students and practitioners with access to online resources, advice and guidance on the use of information technology, including JISC TechDiS (an advisory service on technologies for inclusion), and 12 regional support centres across the UK.
Vital	www.vital.ac.uk	Vital is a professional development programme delivered by The Open University and partially funded by the Department for Education. Vital aims to support practitioners in sharing their expertise to enhance the quality of teaching and learning. Activities and resources include subject and special interest portals, case studies, lesson ideas and a range of online and face-to-face events.

success. Consider learners born in the year 2000, who will now be embarking on their high school experience. These learners only know a world with high-speed broadband connections, digital television and multimedia, mobile and wireless devices, collaborative online services and networking. How does this exposure shape students' expectations in educational environments, led and facilitated by those influenced but not necessarily brought up on a digital diet?

The use of learning technologies in primary school classrooms will also undoubtedly shape their expectations throughout their secondary, post-compulsory and higher educational experiences. If an institution fails to effectively harness technologies to enhance the learner journey, what impact will this have? As further and higher education become more commercialized, the use of learning technologies may well become an ever more influencing factor in the perceived value and attractiveness of an institution, particularly as tuition fees increase!

Reflection point

- Do you feel under pressure to use technology in your sessions in order to meet learners' expectations?
- Do you feel that some use of technology is driven by a desire to entertain or compete with colleagues?

The true extent of any such digital divides and subsequent pedagogical considerations for practitioners is still the focus of much ongoing debate (see Thomas 2011), with a number of emerging claims that the reality of differences in technology use between adults and young people is much more diverse than the native–immigrant dichotomy presents. A range of empirical research has attempted to explore whether there really is a homogenous generational preference in technology use (see Lohnes and Kinzer 2007; Guo et al. 2008; Bullen et al. 2011; Margaryan et al. 2011), with few conclusions to support a clear difference in the way those born since 1980 adopt technology in their approach to learning.

Bennett et al. (2008) argue that the research on young people's relationships with technology is much more complex than the digital native characterization may suggest. One such complexity is the divide between the digital 'haves' and the 'have nots', in terms of access to technology, which raises important considerations around access and inclusion (Hughes 2009: 6; Holley and Oliver 2011).

So what is the general trend?

Certainly the general trend in access to the internet and device ownership has seen large and rapid growth. Market intelligence from the UK communications regulator Ofcom (2011) confirms that the majority of UK homes are now connected to the internet (25 per cent in 2000, 76 per cent in 2011), with nine out of ten people now owning a mobile phone (36 per cent in 2000, 91 per cent in 2011). A quarter of adults (27 per cent) and almost half of teenagers (47 per cent) own a smartphone, and around 28 per cent of UK adults use their mobile phones for internet access. Ofcom's research also identifies a high level of reported addiction to the use of mobile devices, with 37 per cent of adults and 60 per cent of teens admitting they are highly addicted, including over a fifth of adult and nearly half of teenage smartphone users who admitted using or answering their handset in the bathroom or toilet!

We are now ever more able to access and interact with the Web on the go, from blogging on the train, checking emails in the bank queue, even shopping online while burning calories in the gym. With this very observable pervasiveness, it is easy to forget that many young people from more disadvantaged backgrounds may not have the exposure to the range of technologies that we might expect. The cost of personal computers, smartphones and broadband internet connections have all reduced significantly over the last five years, although for many their expense is not a priority in times of high unemployment, tax rises and benefit cuts.

Despite the growth in device ownership and access to the internet, it is estimated that over 800,000 of the most disadvantaged schoolchildren in the UK, some 10 per cent, still cannot go online at home (e-Learning Foundation 2012). This lack of access to the latest devices or to online services for many learners is problematic and does not facilitate the opportunity for experimentation and familiarization to develop the digital literacies and practices often associated with the network generation. As practitioners, we need to be alert to the disparity in technology access and associated skills development and consider ways that our use of technologies can be inclusive and empowering.

Reflection point

- How would you manage an environment with a great diversity of learners, in terms of digital skills and access to technologies?
- Does the infrastructure in your institution support this diversity, or are the expectations of digital natives unrealistic given limited access to equipment and connectivity?

Find out more

Launched in 2001, the e-Learning Foundation charity aims to ensure that all children have access at home and at school to learning resources to fulfil their potential and overcome disadvantage. Working in partnership with schools, parents, charities and businesses, the Foundation helps schools and families provide computers, educational software and internet access to all schoolchildren, especially those from disadvantaged backgrounds and with special learning needs.

So what do we mean by developing digital wisdom?

The debates around digital divides and the use of the native–immigrant metaphor are ongoing conversations. They raise important considerations and questions for our practice, and provide a useful and timely opportunity to reflect on our own views about the use of technology and to explore and recognize our feelings around confidence, knowledge, skills and abilities.

Reflection point

- When you consider the use of technology in education, what feelings do you identify? Are they positive, negative or mixed?
- Do you feel comfortable with consumer technologies in your social world? How do these skills translate to technology in your professional role?
- Now consider why you may have these feelings. Are they based on current or past experiences?
- Do you feel you are speaking the same language as your learners? Do you feel out of touch, under pressure, or excited to embrace change and emerging developments?

You may have identified a number of different reactions. Perhaps you are reading this text because you feel significant pressure to engage with technology in education due to the changing expectations of your learners, of management or the educational community. Perhaps you feel open to and confident with the use of technology in your teaching but are looking for different applications. Maybe you can identify some benefits to the use of technology in your approaches to learning and assessment but recognize a need to develop more practical skills and to identify aspects of your practice where technology will have a positive pedagogical impact, rather than simply being a 'bolt-on' that looks good or will impress an observer.

Revisiting the relevance of his original distinction between the digitally native learner and immigrant tutor, Prensky (2009) more recently asserts a move towards the recognition of the power of digital enhancement and the need for both learners and their tutors to develop digital wisdom – defined as both the 'wisdom arising from the use of digital technology to access cognitive power beyond our innate capacity and [the] wisdom in the prudent use of technology to enhance our capabilities'. This dual view of wisdom raises important considerations for practitioners in terms of our role.

Certainly, computers have capacity to carry out countless functions and tasks more efficiently and effectively than we would be able to alone. From the pocket calculator to the Google search, everyday technologies transform and enhance the cognitive power of searching and calculating. So is our role to teach ICT competence? Many learners reach today's primary schools with a sophisticated grasp of complex computer technologies, exceeding the capabilities of many schoolteachers! Through experimentation and socialization, many of these young learners feel naturally comfortable and adept at utilizing the power of everyday consumer devices.

However, this view of technologies as simple 'tools for learning', to enhance human cognitive performance, is perhaps one which risks marginalizing other important dimensions of learning, such as the social and cultural. Goodfellow and Lea (2007: 33) suggest thinking of technologies not simply as tools but as 'sites' where various kinds of social practices can be played out for pedagogical benefit. These sites might be locations for collaboration, communication, experimentation, failure and success.

A second view of digital wisdom

The second view of digital wisdom, in how best to use the technologies available to us, raises arguably contentious questions around the role of all educators in the development of learners to be effective and literate 'digital citizens'. Many tutors are comfortable with the view that as well as developing subject knowledge and understanding, their role also includes advice, guidance and correction on the appropriate use of written English, but what of a requirement – and need – to develop digital literacies and wisdom in our learners? You would not ask a maths teacher to teach plumbing, but would you ask all teachers to teach digital wisdom?

The vocational practitioner

Those working with vocational learners in a college environment will be well aware of their responsibilities to develop skills in functional English and maths and to contextualize and embed these skills in work-related contexts. This is a contentious strategy, with many vocational tutors ill-equipped and not prepared to deliver these core skills. Casey et al. (2006) explored the impact of embedded approaches to key skills on

79 vocational programmes. The courses were based in 15 further education colleges and one large training provider located in five regions of England. The study highlighted:

> 'One negative note amongst these findings was that, where a single teacher was asked to take dual responsibility for teaching vocational skills and LLN, the probability of learners succeeding with literacy and numeracy qualifications was lower. Learners were twice as likely to fail in these circumstances' (Casey et al. 2006: 5).

In this changing landscape, adult literacy and numeracy provision is now an established component of vocational education and training in the United Kingdom. It is therefore an essential part of a practitioner's role. Is it now timely to consider digital literacy a key skill that all young people need to develop in order to function effectively in the modern world? Consequently, should the development of these skills and practices also be the responsibility of the vocational practitioner, or indeed all teaching practitioners?

Creative production, critical reading and collaborative knowledge building are arguably digital practices that are required for successful lifelong learning (see Sharpe et al. 2010: 9). So perhaps the tutor's role is changing to one that needs to recognize the existing digital capabilities of some, but not all, of our learners – a role which is crucial in developing these technical skills into digital literacies, where learners develop their identities and wisdom to exploit the cognitive, social and cultural benefits of technology to become effective, articulate and confident citizens of the digital, knowledge age.

> 'In a digital age, learners need to practise and experiment with different ways of enacting their identities, and adopt subject positions through different social technologies and media. These opportunities can only be supported by academic staff who are themselves engaged in digital practices and questioning their own relationships with knowledge.' (Beetham and Oliver 2010: 167)

Technology-enhanced pedagogies

Reflection point

- What is your personal philosophy of education? How do you view the role of an educator?
- Do you describe your role as a tutor, teacher, educator, lecturer or trainer? Are these just titles or do they provide an insight into how we perceive knowledge and view our professional role?

You may have identified a range of different facets to your professional role, such as instructor, designer or facilitator. You may see your role as one of guide, helping learners to navigate the various discourses of their subject specialism, and to access information to support development of their knowledge and construction of meaning and insight. Your role may well depend on the context or contexts in which you practise, the level of study and the nature of the qualifications and educational programmes you teach on. Are your learners required to recall knowledge, demonstrate understanding or acquire specific practical skills?

Considering different approaches to teaching and learning

For many, the more traditional behaviourist and cognitivist theories of learning no longer fully resonate with the real purpose and value of education and our wider role in working most effectively with learners. Rather than the transmission of knowledge from expert to novice, to be recalled and reproduced, more contemporary theories of learning place the learner, not the instructor, at the centre of the educational process, with the role of tutor to guide and support learners as they actively develop their ability to make meaning and construct deeper understanding.

Rather than communicating an objectivist view of knowledge, constructivist learning theories recognize the central role of the learner in constructing their own knowledge and dynamic understanding of the world through their own interactions and lived experiences. Education becomes a process of supporting learners in constructing their own meaning based on their prior experiences, through interpretation, accommodation, assimilation and socialization. The role of education therefore becomes one of scaffolding and supporting this process of personalized knowledge construction. Social constructivist theory acknowledges the role of others and the importance of social interaction in developing understanding, insight and meaning-making.

Harasim (2010: 68) identifies four key principles or values associated with a constructivist view of learning:

1   active learning
2   learning by doing
3   scaffolded learning
4   collaborative learning.

Practitioners who have been trained in more recent years will be very familiar with these concepts as the dominant pedagogies of the current age, which form a significant underpinning component of any teacher training programme. Getting learners to actively participate in their learning through experiential tasks is often regarded as an effective pedagogy as this engages learners to work together in their construction of knowledge and understanding – reinforcing, consolidating and applying. The support of the tutor and peers are also seen as key in scaffolding and stretching the development of learners.

Holmes and Gardner (2006) use the term 'communal constructivism' to describe how learners are increasingly using e-learning technologies to create new learning for themselves, but also to contribute and store this learning in a communal knowledge base for the benefit of their community's existing and new learners.

This could be seen where learners actively contribute to discussion forums on a virtual learning environment or public website, or via a blog or wiki. The power of networked learning allows learners to shape their online experience, making a contribution and constructing learning with others through an online community.

Reflection point

- Discussions, collaborative tasks, problem-based learning and peer assessment are undoubtedly common features of many modern learning environments, but how can the use of technology support a constructivist and social constructivist pedagogical approach?

What is Web 2.0?

The online sites of Facebook, YouTube, Twitter and the blogging service WordPress all feature regularly in the world's most visited web pages. They are often categorized as part of the 'Web 2.0' generation of internet applications, and all involve active collaboration, communication and contribution by users.

> 'Web 2.0 is the network as platform, spanning all connected devices. Web 2.0 applications are those that make the most of the intrinsic advantages of that platform: delivering software that gets better the more people use it… going beyond the page metaphor of Web 1.0 to deliver rich user experiences.' (O'Reilly 2005)

In terms of services, Web 2.0 is often defined as an umbrella term which encompasses more recent internet applications that facilitate social interaction, such as podcasting, video sharing, wikis, data mash-ups, virtual societies, social networking, blogging and online gaming (Anderson 2007; Selwyn 2008; Pang 2009). Web 2.0 characterized a significant shift in the democratization of the internet, from a web largely controlled by those skilled in coding and website authoring, to a platform which allows any user not only to read but to actively create, shape and collaborate with the Web – anytime, anyplace.

This shift from so-called Web 1.0 to Web 2.0 did not materialize overnight but as a result of continued technological advances which demanded a dynamic web that shapes and is shaped by its users. Web 2.0 services arguably support and facilitate the principles of a social constructivist learning pedagogy, allowing users locally and worldwide to come together in the active and experiential process of sharing, construction and deconstruction of knowledge and understanding.

Connectivism as a learning theory

The impact of technological developments and their facilitation of an online, connected and collaborative digital, knowledge age are prompting some to identify new theories of learning and associated pedagogies. Siemens (2005) suggests 'connectivism' as one response to the limitations of existing learning theories.

> 'These theories do not address learning that occurs outside of people (learning that is stored and manipulated by technology). They also fail to describe how learning happens within organizations.' (Siemens 2005)

He proposes connectivism as a theory which acknowledges that actionable knowledge (learning) can reside outside of ourselves, for example within an organization or a database, and that decisions are based on rapidly altering foundations as new information is continually acquired. As learners connected to others via sophisticated online networks, we are able to acquire new information rapidly and almost continuously. He highlights the need for learners in an online digital age to be able to draw distinctions between important and unimportant information.

Principles of connectivism (Siemens 2005):

- Learning and knowledge rests in diversity of opinions.
- Learning is a process of connecting specialized nodes or information sources.
- Learning may reside in non-human appliances.
- Capacity to know more is more critical than what is currently known.

- Nurturing and maintaining connections is needed to facilitate continual learning.
- Ability to see connections between fields, ideas, and concepts is a core skill.
- Currency (accurate, up-to-date knowledge) is the intent of all connectivist learning activities.
- Decision making is itself a learning process. Choosing what to learn and the meaning of incoming information is seen through the lens of a shifting reality. While there is a right answer now, it may be wrong tomorrow due to alterations in the information climate affecting the decision.

Online collaborative learning as a theory for a digital age

Harasim (2010: 81) proposes online collaborative learning (OCL) theory as a framework to guide and enhance conventional classroom and distance education. No longer in an industrial age, OCL recognizes the need for a theory of learning that emphasizes knowledge work, knowledge creation and knowledge community. OCL focuses on collaborative learning, knowledge building and internet use as a 'means to reshape formal, non-formal and informal education'.

> 'Ours is a knowledge-creating age and our theories and practice of learning are challenged to move beyond didactic and even active learning approaches to enable learners to become knowledge builders' (Harasim 2010: 89).

Reflection point

- What are your underlying beliefs about knowledge (epistemology)? Does your current approach to teaching and learning focus on the transmission of information or on the creation of an active learning environment which helps learners to construct their own knowledge and understanding?
- Do you feel that so-called Web 2.0 technologies have the potential to enhance a constructivist and social-constructivist approach?

Living and learning technologies

The popularity of online social media sites is clear through the exponential rise in engagement as demonstrated by the number of users. However, not all of our learners will be active users, and indeed some may be actively removing themselves from online connectivity, due to the constant pressures to keep up with and contribute to online communities. While much of the literature seeks to explore the digital divide and suggest recommendations to close the 'gap' between the use and adoption of technology by natives and immigrants, Waycott et al. (2009) and Caruso and Kvavik (2005) suggest that a clear distinction between 'living' (social) and 'learning' technologies is actually an appropriate divide, welcomed by many students. They often see instant messaging and social networking sites as within the scope of their personal lives and there they should remain!

The boundaries of formal and informal learning are becoming increasingly blurred. While this is a welcome development for many, we need to be conscious that the deconstruction of these boundaries, facilitated by pervasive technologies which transcend timetables, physical meetings and the scheduled tutorial, may prompt a serious reconsideration of our working patterns and working practices as tutors.

Reflection point

- Should education try and harness the benefits of living technologies, such as popular social media sites?
- Do you know how your own learners view the technologies they use on a daily basis, and would they be happy for tutors to use these for educational objectives?

Twenty-first-century educators: what is our role in responding to the changes?

These continued discussions raise many questions for those involved in the teaching and learning of young people and how the development of technology affects what, how and who we teach. Whether we identify ourselves as digital natives, immigrants, tourists, settlers or visitors, it seems reasonable to conclude that the use of both living and learning technologies, particularly by younger students, is becoming ever more prolific, although the recognition of a distinct set of learning preferences for a homogenous 'network' generation appears much more complex.

Enhancing the best of traditional approaches

The view of online learning technologies as 'sites for learning', rather than tools, may focus our attention less on the use of the latest gimmick or gadget than on the more general power of technology to enhance our existing epistemological and pedagogical practice. The use of technology alone does not make an outstanding teacher or an outstanding lesson. Learners may well be entertained, but it may not have a positive impact on their learning outcomes.

Higgins et al. (2011) highlight the importance of supplementing, rather than replacing, tried and tested traditional approaches to teaching and learning that are still effective. Thinking about the way you use the technology, rather than about the technology itself, can help to keep the focus on the pedagogy and its impact for learning and learners.

One of the challenges of the twenty-first-century practitioner is to find a balance of practice: one where technology enhances the most effective traditional pedagogical approaches, such as feedback, assessment for learning and reflection. Achieving this balance is not easy but will help to ensure that our new millennium learners are actively and effectively engaged with their learning experiences and better prepared to be effective and wise digital citizens.

Reflection point

- How can we move to a more balanced practice, where we augment the best aspects of our existing traditional practice with the benefits of technology?

The changing role of tutors in a digital age

Drawing on their experiences of corporate training in global businesses, Campbell and Finegan (2011) advocate an adaption of traditional, formalized learning strategies, that target those who learn independently and in isolation from technology, to strategies that recognize that today's learners are connected to an extensive network of people and information that will be continuously used as a learning and problem-solving resource.

They identify a new emerging 'species' of learner, the 'Social Cyborg', which they characterize as those learners who have integrated social networks and information communication technology into the way they think, learn and solve problems. They suggest an evolution in learning strategies, tool sets, skill sets, and mindset to serve the needs of Cyborg learners.

Campbell and Finegan (2011) view the changing role of educators as *learning catalysts*, rather than content designers and deliverers. Siemens (2008: 15) provides an overview of three alternative metaphors proposed by educators (see Table 1.2), which reflect the changing role of educators in a digital age: the educator as 'master artist' (Seely Brown 2009), 'concierge' (Bonk 2007) and as 'curator' (Siemens 2008).

So what does this mean to you as a practitioner?

It could be viewed that in the twenty-first century our role is one of 'educator as gardener'; we need to provide the conditions suitable for growth. We need to nurture and support, while giving room for development. We cannot ultimately control the outputs but we can lay good foundations to promote germination and propagation of knowledge.

The gardener uses technology to protect fragile new growth. The greenhouse, the heating, the nutrients and the lighting work together to enhance the traditional components of earth, light and water.

Table 1.2 Metaphors for educators in a digital age

Metaphor	Real-world role	Educator role
Educator as master artist (Seely Brown)	In the open environment of the art studio, artists develop their craft while the 'master' can highlight examples of emerging good practice. Students work alongside each other, absorbing and influenced by the developing works of fellow creators around them.	In open and collaborative online environments, such as forums, discussion boards and blogs, learners can view each other's contributions and observe their developing creations. The tutor is able to view and comment on individual posts, highlighting emerging good practice or points of particular merit.
Educator as concierge (Bonk)	The hotel concierge guides and helps new visitors to get the most out of their experience. They provide expert advice, support and insight into places of interests and 'hidden gems'. They can signpost visitors to sites that will best meet their objectives.	The online educator can similarly highlight interesting sites of educational discovery, directing learners to information sources and experiences, and promote exploration and collaboration. The tutor, as expert, can signpost learners to hidden gems amongst the plethora of online information and data.
Educator as curator (Siemens)	Curators are experts in their field, with a sound knowledge of their specialist domain. They manage the presentation of artefacts and displays, enabling visitors to freely explore while assisting them in gaining a useful insight into this specialist field.	The educator is both subject expert, able to present concepts, ideas, histories and artefacts, and also a guide, to foster and promote learners' own exploration, independent discovery and connection making.

(Based on Siemens 2008: 15–17)

Or perhaps our role is similar to that of a space agency – to prepare our learners for exploration of an unknown world. Learners will be employed in jobs that may not even exist yet, solving problems that we don't yet know we have and using technologies that are yet to be realized. We cannot give these learners the answers because we do not yet know the questions.

What we do know is that today's learners will need to be confident and digitally literate in order to effectively operate and influence their digital world of tomorrow. We can develop their independence, criticality, resourcefulness and wisdom in utilizing all the tools available to them, to meet the objectives they are faced with. But does the current educational landscape support this approach?

When we look at the current summative assessment model of the dominant examinations system taken by the majority of young people in the UK, does a two-hour unseen examination in a cold gym hall really reflect the real-life skills required in a digital world? At what other moment in that learner's life will they ever be presented with a situation that requires them to recall knowledge and demonstrate comprehension without access to any type of network?

Reflection point

- What is your view of the role of the twenty-first-century educator? Do you see yourself as curator, artist, concierge, conductor, director or gardener?
- How does your educational experience equip learners with the skills and wisdom to function in an unknown digital society?

Multimodal and multimedia

Preparing young and older learners to meet the challenges of the future is a vital part of education. For most of them, that future will include having access to, understanding and using a wide-ranging assortment of information and communication technologies, including those that are familiar today as well as those not yet imagined. We would suggest that the way knowledge is represented, as well as the mode and media chosen, is a vital aspect of knowledge construction, making the form of representation essential to meaning and learning more generally. That is, the ways in which something is represented shapes both what is to be learned, including the content of the curriculum, and how it is to be learned.

To have a stronger understanding of learning and teaching in the multimodal environment of the contemporary classroom is quintessential when exploring the means in which representations in all modes feature in the classroom. The focus here, then, is on multimodality on the representations and the learning potentials of teaching materials and the ways in which teachers and learners utilize these through their engagement in and out of the classroom.

Multimodal approaches to teaching and learning

You can provide stimulating and exciting multimodal texts to encourage your learners to write. This can be a tool to help develop learners' confidence. For example, those who have previously avoided writing may record their voices via audio or film their narration after practising their stories with a peer. This allows the learners the opportunity to be creative and work in a mode that suits them and promotes learning.

Quality teaching and learning can be enriched when focus is given to the development of dynamic ICT-rich learning experiences. Multimodal teaching and learning environments using a range of new communication technologies can therefore enhance the teaching and the learning experience for our learners.

A multimodal approach to the use of teaching tools, activities and resources can be considered within a wider cultural shift away from written text to the use of images, sound, and so on. Within this, the role of the practitioner in encouraging learners' participation involves the tutors' 'shaping', or orchestration, of the numerous modes and resources used to support.

Reflection point

- As a learner, have you ever felt that you were a really good learner but not necessarily in the way learning took place when you were in school, college or university?
- Did school, college or university make you sometimes feel stupid?

Why use multimodality?

Many learners feel that the 'fit' between the way they are required to learn and the way they feel they learn best is problematic or incompatible, and because of this many of us also feel that we must not be very intelligent and are lacking the skills and knowledge to be successful in our lives. We need to respect the fact that learners arrive in the classroom with eclectic processes for integrating information. We also need to identify and acknowledge the evidence that young and older learners have distinct modes of self-expression. A multimodal approach to teaching and assessment is a coherent pedagogical approach. From a multimodal perspective, image, action and so forth are referred to as modes, as organized sets of semiotic resources for making meaning. One problem inherent in a lecture-driven, rote form of teaching is the difficulty in assessing learners' actual level of comprehension. In practice, a multimodal approach to teaching offers learners the opportunity to discover truths about the subject being studied on their own, in their own natural learning style.

There are many ways to learn

The more different ways you learn something, the more you really learn it. Multiple modes to teaching and learning can reinforce the learning. In addition to breaking up the monotony, presenting the same concepts in more than one mode can reinforce ideas and help students learn in ways that suit them best.

Reflection point

- Do you currently embrace a multimodal approach to teaching and learning in your professional practice?
- Consider how and why you might embed multimodal approaches into your lessons, seminars or workshops.

You may have identified that you can include web pages, animated PowerPoint presentations or a video or YouTube clip.

You may have identified a variety of different motivations for these approaches, such as:

- enabling you to draw on the learners' interests and hobbies
- to motivate and engage the learners
- to recognize the learning preferences of your group
- as a dynamic approach which models diverse ways of using technology
- to develop a transferable skill which learners can take into their home or work life
- to make the lesson more dynamic and interactive.

The development of multimodality is evolving at a rapid pace. As we write this book, rapid changes are taking place, both within the educational landscape and in the development of technologies. It is very difficult to keep up with these changes, as hard as we try. Indeed, we would argue that we are currently in a transition stage where educational policy and curriculum documents have not yet adapted to changes that have occurred with the range of digital media that are becoming embedded in people's daily lives. For example, new technologies are fundamentally changing literacy practices in contexts outside school, college, and university. The notion of what constitutes 'literacy' has shifted over time, from the decoding of words where it is placed in the realm of an *individual, cognitive skill* to that of literacy as a *social practice* (Street 1984; Barton 1994; Gee 1996; Barton and Hamilton 1998).

Promoting digital literacies

Literacy practices shape the way we relate to and interact with literacy, and are interwoven with our identity and practices. Gee (2000) explores how discourses offer us markers of identity which can shift from one context to the next. New Literacy Studies (NLS) draws on the literacies from learners' lives. These artefacts are a way to develop a dialogue leading to an analysis of the concrete reality represented by the learners. Multimodal approaches to teaching and learning in the educational context embrace a range of strategies that integrate a number of delivery media, mainly facilitated by the creation of information and communication technologies.

A way to address the above is to move towards a model based on a social approach. Social approaches to literacy are sometimes grouped together under the remit of the New Literacy Studies (Street 1984; Barton 1994; Gee 1996; Barton and Hamilton 1998). Within this complex view of the nature of literacy we can highlight that literacy has many purposes for the learner. It challenges the dominance of the autonomous model, and recognizes how literacy practices vary from one cultural and historical context to another. In the private domain of home and the public domain of formal education, literacy practices, identities and discourse are produced by power and ideology so that literacy is shaped differently in different contexts. This focus can help tutors to shift from a narrow competency-based approach, which separates the literacies from their context, and instead harness the everyday practices learners bring into the classroom.

As such, literacy is not just a technical or neutral skill; it provides a social view which is expanded by treating literacy as not only a social practice but also as a multimodal form of communication. The use of multimodal literacies has expanded the ways we acquire information and understand concepts. Ever since the days of illustrated books and maps, texts have included visual elements for the purpose of conveying information. The contemporary difference is the ease with which we can combine words, images, sound, colour, animation, video and styles of print in tasks so that they are part of our everyday lives and, at least by our youngest generation, often taken for granted as they are immersed in technology.

Many young (and older) people take for granted activities such as participating in Twitter, wikis, blogs or various social networking and sharing sites in order to access and shape information from the Web. They also increasingly engage in virtual environments through gaming or in a virtual world such as 'Second Life'. As such, these virtual contexts are shaping and changing the way people present themselves and the way relationships are developed.

Multimodality recognizes music, images, symbols and other forms as literacy practices. The use of multimodal literacies offers an expansion of the ways learners acquire information and understand concepts. Words, images, sound, colour, animation, video, and styles of print can be combined. This approach moves from a deficit model of literacies, and instead recognizes that 'language, literacy and numeracy involves paying attention first and foremost to the contexts, purposes and practices in which language (spoken and written) and mathematical operations play a part' (Barton et al. 2007: 17). As identified in the Teaching and Learning Research Programme, *Harnessing Everyday Literacies for Student Learning at College* (Ivanic 2008: 1), 'literacy is a significant factor affecting retention, progression and achievement in colleges'. The study identified how the span of literacy practices in college was less than that which the students engaged in in their everyday lives. The literacy practices were driven and captured by a 'washback effect' from assessment regimes. The implications were that the everyday literacy practices of the learners were often invisible and not valued as skills that they could bring into the classroom to support learning in a more holistic way.

So what does this mean to you as a practitioner?

Tutors can use an understanding of literacy as a set of social practices to fine-tune their pedagogy. They can make small changes in practice which aim to make reading and writing on courses more resonant with students' vernacular literacy practices, make the students more aware of reading and writing in their everyday lives which could act as a resource for their learning, make the communicative aspects more explicit and visible, and make the reading and writing on courses more relevant to learning (Ivanic 2008: 3).

Indeed, it is generally thought that recognizing the literacies which learners bring into the classroom is an effective strategy for teaching and learning, because purposeful and meaningful learning builds and expands on learners' prior knowledge and experience to shape and construct new knowledge rather than seeing the learner as an empty vessel ready to be filled by the tutor. Learning is seen as a social activity embedded in particular cultures and contexts, where assessment is based on them demonstrating their competence in achieving the specific learning outcomes.

Demonstration of the achievement of these learning outcomes is situated in the learners' real-life and everyday practices. The teaching and learning resources can be developed by the learner to capture and give meaning to their experience, motivation and aspirations, or co-produced with the tutor (see McNamara 2007; Duckworth 2008; Duckworth 2009; Duckworth and Tummons 2010) rather than arising from a prescriptive preset curriculum.

How we live and the workplace

Technology has fundamentally altered how we live and work as well as how we learn. Not only has the nature of classroom learning changed, but also the very concept of the classroom itself has been redefined. As a result, education's reach now extends far beyond what was once possible or even imaginable. This transformative process will undoubtedly continue. Learners moving from higher education into the world of employment, and individuals re-entering the workforce, are also discovering a workplace that is vastly different from the one they might have entered as recently as a half-decade ago. While it used to be the case that only certain specialized occupations required skills in using technology, this is no longer so. Due to shifts in patterns of employment, many people do not have the same stability of employment or the same length of service with a single employer. The concept of a 'job for life' now seems a thing of the past to many people, many being displaced from traditional to new forms of work. A good example of this is in the implementation of ICT across many industrial sectors. Previously labour-intensive processes have been automated, with ICT changing the nature of work, speed and volume of communication, information and working practices. In 2008, a report by the Teaching and Learning Research Programme (TLRP) identified how the 'demand for knowledge workers rises exponentially in the knowledge economy [and] has resulted in a shift from mechanical Taylorism to digital Taylorism, so that knowledge work becomes portable working knowledge' (Brown et al. 2008: 1).

Innovative teaching practices encompass both pedagogy and technology. The use of new and emerging technology is important in the development of learner-centred learning environments that facilitate both deep subject matter knowledge and skills such as collaboration, communication, problem solving, and self-regulation that learners will need to succeed in the twenty-first century. Our learners will need to be able to constantly adapt to new and emerging technologies and to the literacy practices needed for each progression.

To meet the needs of your learners and prepare them for working and personal life in the twenty-first century, you need to prepare them for the new literacy practices and discourses that have become embedded in online social interaction. More than ever, students need to be able to identify the authenticity and ideology of texts and messages, and to critically evaluate the purpose and audience that specific texts are designed for. With the sophistication possible with designing texts, learners need not only to be able to use and manipulate new technologies but to be able to consider the best way to use them for their own purpose and audience. Developing our own digital wisdom will enhance our digital literacy and empower us to create the learning environment that best prepares our learners for tomorrow's digital future.

Digital futures

The internet is full of data and statistics on current levels of engagement with technology. The increase in users of smartphones and social media particularly has been truly exponential. While it is somewhat difficult to predict the next big phenomenon, it is useful to keep an eye on developing trends, in order that we can maintain our digital wisdom and currency.

Each year, the New Media Consortium Horizon Reports describe the six emerging areas of technology most likely to have a significant impact on education (both higher education and 'K-12' or pre-college primary and secondary education) over the next one to five years. The 2012 reports (Johnson et al. 2012a, 2012b) identify a number of emerging technologies (see Table 1.3) with the potential to enter mainstream use within the next five years.

The growth in users, authors, publishers, collaborators and participators all adds to the sheer weight of online information, which continues to grow at an exponential rate. Our ability as learners and practitioners to cope with so much data is being tested. A Google search today will almost certainly produce an unmanageable list of responses with little time to filter and discriminate the useful from the unnecessary.

'For many of today's undergraduates, the idea of being able to conduct an exhaustive search is inconceivable. Information seems to be as limitless as the universe. And research is one of the most difficult challenges facing students in the digital age.' (Head and Eisenberg 2010)

Table 1.3 Emerging technologies in education

Time to adoption	Higher education	K-12 (pre-college)
One year or less	• Mobile apps • Tablet computing	• Mobile devices and apps • Tablet computing
Two to three years	• Game-based learning • Learning analytics	• Game-based learning • Personal learning environments
Four to five years	• Gesture-based computing • Internet of things	• Augmented reality • Natural user interfaces

Johnson et al. (2012a and 2012b)

Future web

For some, the necessary evolution of the internet comes in the form of Web 3.0, considered to be the 'Semantic Web', a term accredited to the Web's original creator, Tim Berners-Lee (Anderson and Whitelock 2004). Berners-Lee envisaged a world where computers would become capable of analysing all the data on the Web: content, links, and transactions between people and computers. The Semantic Web allows computers to read, 'understand' and make meaning out of information that matters most to an individual, as opposed to simply displaying information (McEneaney 2011; Morris 2011). This may mean that tutors and learners can spend less time sifting through information to find the most useful aspects, and spend more time discussing, collaborating and participating.

Give it a go

One developing example, which uses data to present 'solutions' to users' queries, can be seen in WolframAlpha (www.wolframalpha.com), described as a 'computational knowledge engine'. Compare the results of a simple search with this type of 'smart engine' and Google.

Green (2011) suggests that Web 3.0 is also about a shift in how we interact with the internet, including the *mobile* and the *immersive* Web. The rapid increase in use of internet-connected mobile devices has facilitated a more seamless use of the Web as we move from home, to work, to school, to university. Practitioners have been quick to explore the pedagogical potential of mobile devices for learning ('m-learning'), with considerable ongoing debate (Attewell et al. 2010; Traxler and Wishart 2011).

'The future our students will inherit is one that will be mediated and stitched together by the mobile web, and I think that ethically, we are called on as teachers to teach them how to use these technologies effectively.' (Parry 2011)

Real environments to virtual realities

The immersive nature of the developing Web can also be seen in the growing use and popularity of virtual worlds, augmented reality and 3D environments (Green 2011). Second Life (http://secondlife.com) is perhaps the most well-known social virtual world, offering opportunities for real-time collaboration and social construction of understanding, creativity and immersive interaction for over 20 million users (Dalgarno and Lee 2010; Ellis and Anderson 2011; Ferguson 2011).

Unlike immersive virtual reality (VR), which draws the user away from the real world and onto the screen, augmented reality (AR) enhances the real-world experience by combining an overlay of computer generated materials with physical objects in real time. Accessed through smartphones, personal digital assistants (PDAs) and tablet devices, AR applications (apps) aim to simplify the user's life by bringing virtual information to enhance and augment their perception of, interaction with and understanding of the world around them (Zhou et al. 2008; Carmigniani et al. 2010; Yuen et al. 2011). Figure 1.1 provides a visual representation of this as a continuum.

Figure 1.1 Milgram's Reality–Virtuality Continuum (Milgram and Kishino 1994)

So what does this mean for learning?

The continued development of the online world, including applications, devices and modes of engagement, will undoubtedly have continued implications for teaching, learning and assessment. Intelligent searching may address some of the issues around digital literacy and information management often found with current internet searches. Learners may benefit from knowledge construction, as searches through the Semantic Web use linked data to return a media-rich personalized report, including relevant lecture notes, resources, videos, journal articles, blogs, TV programmes and social networking contributions (Ohler 2008).

Armstrong (2009: 960) highlights the crucial link between the developing technologies of Web 3.0 and literacy, and proposes five critical strategies for teachers and students in preparing for tomorrow's world: the need to become fluent in different registers for reading, writing and communicating in multiple worlds; to become fluent in switching or multitasking; to build on the transferable knowledge of the past; to create and collaborate constantly; and to conceive of work and play as seamless.

Digital concerns

In some respects, Web 3.0 is already here: when we shop online, we are often presented with a series of 'personalized' recommendations based on our previous purchases and searches; when using online music services, our existing tastes and preferences are used to suggest new media that might also be to our taste. But its rapid expansion is not without concerns or barriers. Who will decide how and what information is tagged, will this be 'accurate', and will anyone actually bother?

Ohler (2010: 17) identifies how the unavoidable imposed bias and perspectives of those coding information into the Semantic Web could mean the 'rewriting of the world as we know it' through a subtle but global 'rendering of reality'. Concerns have also been raised around information security and privacy as our personal preferences and online behaviours are tracked and used to filter the responses to our future information needs (Anderson and Whitelock 2004).

So what does this mean to you as a practitioner?

Our role in raising our learners' awareness of issues around information validity, reliability and authenticity looks set to become ever more crucial. Moving on from awareness-raising of plagiarism issues fuelled by the ease of access to online information, learners will need the skills to evaluate all information sources for appropriateness, as well as how to reference these sources appropriately.

Online safety and security are also areas where our support and guidance may need to be focused and enhanced as we develop a digital wisdom fit for the next generation of the Web. Our digital footprints can leave significant tracks, and our professional profiles may become compromised as the blurring between professional and private lives lived out online merge closer together. Who can see your Facebook profile, its images, your postings and history? What 'tweets' are your learners posting and who is following them? The possibility and ease of online publication is empowering, but difficult to erase.

The open education movement

Another area which is gathering momentum is the notion of 'open educational resources' (OER) and the wider 'open education movement', often relating to open licensing, open access, open formats, open resources and open software. Through the power of technology, we are seeing an increasingly rapid shift in the democratization of educational content, to allow more people than ever before to access valuable resources without the financial barriers (see Table 1.4). It will be interesting to watch the development of the open movement, facilitated globally through technology and online access, and its resulting impact on learning and learners.

'Open education is about sharing, reducing barriers and increasing access in education. It includes free and open access to platforms, tools and resources in education (such as learning materials, course materials, videos of lectures, assessment tools, research, study groups, textbooks, etc.). Open education seeks to create a world in which the desire to learn is fully met by the opportunity to do so, where everyone, everywhere is able to access affordable, educationally

Table 1.4 Open education examples

Jorum www.jorum.ac.uk	An example of open educational resource sharing, Jorum is a JISC-funded online repository providing free access for UK further and higher education providers to hundreds of learning and teaching materials across a range of subjects, which can be reused and repurposed.
Apache OpenOffice www.openoffice.org	OpenOffice is an example of open-source software. It offers users a range of office software for word processing, spreadsheets, presentations, graphics and databases. Available in many languages, OpenOffice works on all common computers and can be downloaded and used completely free of charge for any purpose.
Research in Learning Technology www.researchinlearningtechnology.net	*Research in Learning Technology* is the international, quarterly, peer-reviewed journal of the Association for Learning Technology and is an example of open access (OA) literature. The journal provides barrier-free access to current and previous articles which aim to research and share good practice in the use of learning technologies.
Creative Commons www.creativecommons.org.uk	Founded in the United States in 2001, Creative Commons is a non-profit corporation which provides free licences and tools to allow content creators to share their work for others to use and remix, while retaining their copyright. A range of different licensing options are available.
Coursera www.coursera.org	Coursera is a social entrepreneurship company working in partnership with some of the world's top universities to offer free online courses in a range of subjects, from statistics to health care. Coursera aims to provide millions of learners worldwide with access to world-class education through the power of online technology.

and culturally appropriate opportunities to gain whatever knowledge or training they desire.' (www.openeducationweek.org 2012)

Find out more

To find out more about the open education movement, you may wish to explore the 'infokit' provided by JISC: https://openeducationalresources.pbworks.com

The OpenCourseWare Consortium (www.ocwconsortium.org) is a group of higher education institutions and associated organizations committed to advancing 'OpenCourseWare' and its impact on global education. In May 2012, the consortium organized the first Open Education Week to raise awareness of the open education movement and its impact on teaching and learning worldwide. For more information, visit: www.openeducationweek.org

In financially austere times, there is also an increasing trend for institutions to facilitate the growth of the 'bring your own device' (BYOD) movement. We all know how to use our own mobile phones, tablets and notebooks. Our own devices are becoming increasingly personalized to reflect our own preferences, layouts and software. The ability to quickly and easily connect to institutional networks with our devices is attractive, if perhaps problematic to some network technicians! Concerns over network security have hampered many large-scale BYOD initiatives, although these barriers are broken down as the significant financial and productivity advantages are realized.

Find out more

'eduroam' (education roaming) is a secure worldwide roaming access service developed for the international research and education community. Starting in Europe in 2003, eduroam now allows students, researchers and staff in over 54 countries to obtain internet connectivity when visiting other participating educational institutions.

Click: www.eduroam.org

Digital updating

We recognize that any publication on technology and learning needs to be sensitive to the rapid and dynamic pace of change and development. For practitioners, perhaps our biggest challenge is finding time and space to keep up with these developments, juggling with our day-to-day commitments and responsibilities.

The use of technology should be our friend and guide in this process too. Technology has the ability to stream information relevant to us into user-friendly interfaces. In Table 1.5 we propose a number of locations of interest that might be your first port of call in maintaining your digital currency.

Table 1.5 Keeping digitally updated

Twitter www.twitter.com	The microblogging site is a great way to receive bite-sized updates with links to meaningful information. Sign up for free and follow the movers and shakers in the technology-enhanced learning world. Their daily tweets will offer you an exciting menu of the latest research findings, the devices and software for use in your practice. Browse on your mobile device over lunch, in the post office queue or on the train home.
Education Eye from Futurelab www.educationeye.org.uk	A free online space that provides easy access to a range of relevant and useful innovations selected from the Web each day. The Eye provides a way to discover, explore and share new ideas, mapping educational websites, forums and practitioner case studies.
Centre for Learning and Performance Technologies (C4LPT) http://c4lpt.co.uk	Founded by social media consultant and writer Jane Hart, the Centre for Learning and Performance Technologies (C4LPT) is a free resource site on the use of new technologies for learning and performance. C4LPT includes a tools directory, including the top 100 tools for learning, as voted for each year by educators around the world, and the Social Learning Centre, an online space for learning professionals to connect and learn from their peers.
Mary Meeker's Internet Trends www.kpcb.com/insights/2012-internet-trends	Keep abreast of general worldwide internet trends with renowned American analyst Mary Meeker's annual report. The analysis reflects the commercial world and is useful in considering how changes will be felt in the educational landscape.

RSS feeds

 RSS stands for 'Really Simple Syndication'. An RSS feed is basically a web page which is read by a reader on your computer to stream the latest news from a specific website. RSS feeds are useful to keep up with the latest updates from specific organizations. Look for the orange RSS logo on your favourite sites. **Click**: www.feedzilla.com

Personalized dashboards

Just finding the time to keep up to date with the daily updates from the Web is a challenge in itself for a busy practitioner.

Personalized home pages or dashboards, such as netvibes and iGoogle, can provide a 'one-stop shop' for all your information needs and feeds.

Your Twitter updates, blogs, social networks and favourite websites can all be presented on one page, to save you time logging in, remembering passwords and accessing multiple sites.

Click: www.netvibes.com; www.google.com/ig

Technology Enhanced Learning (www.tel.ac.uk) is a £12 million multi-project programme exploring how technology can be designed and built so that it improves learning:

- Designing and evaluating systems to advance our understanding of learning and teaching in a technological context.
- Supporting eight large interdisciplinary projects.
- Working to achieve impact for emerging research results.
- Mapping progress on key themes.

Findings of the TEL programme

System Upgrade: Realising the Vision for UK Education (Noss et al. 2012) is a report summarizing the findings of the TEL programme in the wider context of technology-enhanced learning. Addressing 12 key themes, as presented in Table 1.6, the report offers 12 useful recommendations for all educators looking to get the very best out of technology for learning.

Table 1.6   *System Upgrade: Realising the Vision for UK Education* (2012) A report from the ESRC/EPSRC Technology Enhanced Learning research programme. Director: Richard Noss, London Knowledge Lab.

Theme	Recommendation
Connect	Exploit the power of personal devices to enhance learning
Share	Catch the wave of social networking to share ideas and learn together
Analyse	Use technology to understand better how we learn, and so help us learn better
Assess	Develop technologies to assess what matters, rather than what is easy to assess
Apply	Allow technology to help learners apply their education to the real world
Personalize	Utilize artificial intelligence to personalize teaching and learning
Engage	Go beyond the keyboard and mouse to learn through movement and gesture
Streamline	Enhance teachers' productivity with new tools for designing teaching and learning
Include	Empower the digitally and socially excluded to learn with technology
Know	Employ tools to help learners make sense of the information overload
Compute	Understand how computers think, to help learners shape the world around them
Construct	Unleash learners' creativity through building and tinkering

Reflecting on digital practice

Reflection point

- What does reflection mean to you?
- How do you reflect as a teaching practitioner?
- What actions do you take as a result of your reflections?

The importance for all teaching professionals of continually reflecting and re-evaluating their practice is a generally well-recognized and regarded practice (see Moon 1999; Hillier 2002; Rhodes et al. 2004). Reflection allows us to step back, review our actions, and consider what went well, what might be improved and how we might go about enhancing our future practice.

> 'Good teachers are by definition reflective practitioners ... they are relentless about striving for improvement in their practice, they challenge and question themselves, they look for new and improved ways of working so that all their learners are enabled to make the best possible progress.'
> (Rhodes et al. 2004: 55)

Reflecting 'in' and 'on' action

The work and models of Dewey (1933), Schön (1983), Kolb (1984) and Brookfield (1995) have all influenced the manner in which 'reflection' is viewed and carried out. Building on Dewey's work, Schön (1983) proposes two forms of reflective practice, 'reflection-in-action' and 'reflection-on-action', in order that professionals are able to explore their experiences and what they know, with a view to becoming more effective, more creative and more 'professional' in their work.

Reflection-in-action 'involves thinking about action while actually executing it, which may result in modification to the action while it is in progress' (Schön 1983: 50). For the tutor, reflection-in-action could be the modification of a well-prepared lesson to meet the needs of the learners. Perhaps the learners have more prior knowledge of a particular topic than anticipated, or perhaps the behaviour of the group is much more disruptive than predicted. In these cases, the 'effective tutor' is able to draw on their experience, knowledge, skills and understanding of these and other situations – 'what Schön calls the professional "repertoire"' (Tummons 2007: 74) – and is able to change direction and run the session in a different, more effective way.

Post-event reflections could be seen as 'reflection-on-action'. Reflection-on-action 'involves thinking back and talking about action, which may result in subsequent actions of a similar type being modified in the light of such reflection' (Schön 1983: 50). For the tutor, this could be the post-lesson evaluation process, where a critical reflection of the session is carried out in terms of effectiveness of teaching and learning strategies, learner participation and engagement, inclusivity and environmental factors, to name a few.

Models to guide reflective practice

Arguably the trainee teacher's most common introduction to the notions of reflection and reflective practice come from Kolb's (1984) 'experiential learning cycle'. Used widely throughout teacher education programmes, Kolb's cycle of experiential learning is a circle in which 'reflective observation' is the process of bringing the 'concrete experience' of events or experiences to the state of 'abstract conceptualization'. These abstract concepts can then be 'tested' in the further stage of 'active experimentation'.

Gibbs (1988) offers a model for reflection or a 'reflection cycle' based on the work of Kolb. Gibb's six-stage model provides a useful framework when reflecting on 'concrete experiences' such as lessons, either face to face or online, for example: 'description – what happened?'; 'feelings – what were you thinking and feeling?'; 'evaluation – what was good and bad about the experience?'; 'analysis – what sense can you make of the situation?'; 'conclusion – what else could you have done?'; and 'action plan – if it arose again, what would you do?'

A further model of reflection which considers multiple perspectives is provided by Brookfield (1995), who introduces the notion of 'critical lenses for reflection'. Brookfield argued that reflection is something to be encouraged amongst learners as well as tutors. He identifies four different points of view, or critical

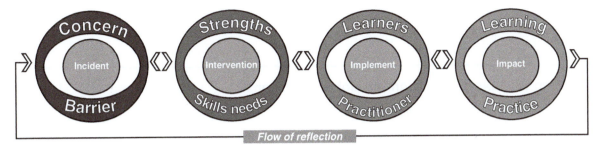

Figure 1.2   The IRIS model

lenses, which should be taken into consideration when reflecting on practice: autobiography; learners' eyes; colleagues' perceptions; and theoretical, philosophical and research literature. This could be interpreted as an appreciation and recognition of the point of view of the practitioner, the point of view of our learners, the point of view of our colleagues, and the point of view of established theory.

A new model for reflection

Acknowledging the benefits of all these models of reflection, we propose our own interpretation of the reflective process with the 'Independent Reflective Investigation for Solution(s)' model (IRIS) (see Figure 1.2). The IRIS lens of reflection encourages a solutions-based approach to addressing barriers or concerns in professional practice. Four sequential lenses are presented to guide reflectors to consider how their existing strengths and ongoing skills development can be used to identify an intervention. The model encourages users to move through the flow of reflection, focusing on how interventions may be implemented practically and what impact they may have on both future practice and learning outcomes.

Stage 1: Incident

Identify a particular critical incident from your practice or experience to reflect on. Describe the incident – what is, or are, your concerns? Have you identified a barrier to success?

Stage 2: Intervention

Having identified an incidence of your practice, consider an intervention that might address your concerns. How can this intervention build on your existing strengths? What skills might you need to develop, and who could support you to move through the flow?

Stage 3: Implement

Having identified a possible intervention, how might you practically implement this in your practice? What could both you and the learners do to make it happen? What practical and logistical considerations do you need to address?

Stage 4: Impact

Now consider what impact the intervention might have on your practice, on the learners and on your pedagogy. What would success look like? Are there any areas of risk? How will you measure the impact? Was the implementation successful? Do you have any further concerns?

Depending on the outcome, reflectors can return to each stage of the model to refine and develop their reflections and their practice.

An example of reflection through the IRIS lens

(Reena, an FE lecturer in public services)

Stage 1: Incident

Some of the learners in my BTEC group can be disruptive and have a short attention span. When I am going through a PowerPoint presentation, they can sometimes lose focus and start chatting. I get frustrated trying to keep them on task. They need this information to be able to complete their assignments.

Stage 2: Intervention

I have heard about a PowerPoint protocol called Pecha Kucha which a colleague has used to good effect in her teaching. It is a short presentation that might maintain the interest of my learners. I am quite skilled with PowerPoint but I would need to get help with adding animation and automatic slide transitions. Perhaps a YouTube clip would help.

Stage 3: Implement

I will create a slideshow using the Pecha Kucha principles for an upcoming new unit on health and safety. I will show it in the first lesson to introduce the new topic and then I will ask my learners to work in groups to create their own short presentations on different aspects of health and safety legislation.

Stage 4: Impact

The presentation might keep the learners' interest and get them motivated to work collaboratively on the new topic. Pecha Kucha is only six minutes 40 seconds, so I now spend less time talking and more time helping to facilitate their learning.

They might not understand what they have to do. I will need to monitor this carefully.

Metareflection point

- Throughout this chapter, we have proposed a number of areas for personal reflection. Reflecting on your reflections, do you feel the process has helped you to personalize some of the debates raised and what it means for you and your practice?
- How often do you usually reflect? Is this a formal or informal process? Do you use any models of reflection to guide you through a sequence of steps?
- How might you use technology to help you reflect in the future – for example, blogs, Twitter (microreflections) and online collaboration?

Final thoughts

We have presented and discussed some of the theoretical and philosophical debates on the use of technology to both mediate and enhance learning. We have outlined the role of multimodal and multimedia approaches in reaching out to learners in accessible and creative ways.

We have encouraged you to reflect on these debates and to link theory to your own practice in whichever setting you currently practice. We recognize that learners, institutions and learning environments are incredibly diverse across the lifelong learning sector. What works for one practitioner may be inappropriate for another. What empowers, motivates and engages one group of learners may distract and confuse another. In Part Two, we present a range of technology tools for your consideration. We ask you to explore each in relation to your own situation, drawing on the reflections you have made here and consider how these might add value to your current and future practice. It is important to consider the future and to identify how technology tools can also inform and empower you as a practitioner in a digital, knowledge age. Developing extensive professional social networks is one way of staying connected, informed and digitally wise to choose the right tools to enhance your pedagogy.

PART TWO
Creative technologies: practical ideas for harnessing technology in teaching, learning and assessment

In this section we present a broad range of technology 'tools' for your teaching, learning and assessment toolkit. A number of applied ideas for how you might use these tools to enhance your practice are also included.

It may be useful to keep returning to this section as you develop your skills and consider different ways to harness the advantages technology can bring to your delivery, support and assessment practice and for the outcomes of learners.

By the end of this section, you will have considered:

- What are some of the technology tools I could use in my approach to teaching, learning and assessment?
- How can I use these tools appropriately to meet learning objectives and improve outcomes for my learners?
- Where can I access these technologies to start experimenting and finding out for myself?
- What specific considerations do I need to think about when using these tools with learners in my practice?
- How are other practitioners using these tools with their learners in their own contexts? What can I learn from them?
- Where can I go to find out further information?

Many of the tools we have selected are web-based and free to educational users. We believe that to be most effective, the busy practitioner needs a broad selection of options that:

- are freely available
- are intuitive and easy to use
- are engaging and motivating for learners
- enable learners to work and communicate together
- allow practitioners to use learner-centred teaching techniques.

Each tool is presented with a common structure:

What is it?

This provides an outline of the tool in simple language for the non-technical user.

How could I use it?

Having gained initial ideas about what the tool can do, we present some ideas for how you might use it in your daily practice. We explore potential uses by tutors, by learners, individually and collaboratively.

Where can I find it?

Here we provide links to the tools and how you can begin to quickly access each technology.

Anything I need to consider?

Before using these tools in your practice, we identify any general considerations that would be useful to reflect on before implementation. Different organizations have different policies, procedures and restrictions regarding web-based content, for example. Those working with younger or more vulnerable learners may have specific considerations around e-safety and the moderation of online content.

Give it a go!

The best way to familiarize yourself with the power of each tool is simply to give it a go. Experimentation is strongly recommended to understand how a tool works and how much development might be needed to use it with your learners. We present a range of quick and easy initial activities to get you started.

What are others doing?

Here we provide practical applied ideas and insights into what other practitioners are doing to enhance their teaching, learning and assessment practice. Schoolteachers, college tutors and university lecturers explain how they are harnessing the benefits of technology to motivate, engage, enthuse and include their learners.

Find out more

Some of the tools and ideas may not be appropriate for your own subject, institution or learners, or you may wish to know much more about a tool than we can present here. We identify sources of further advice and guidance where you can dig deeper to explore other uses or similar tools.

Reflection point

We also encourage you to reflect on each tool following experimentation, to consider how and why you might use it in your practice – using it yourself, with your colleagues or used by your learners. You may find the 'IRIS' reflective model helpful in selecting a tool which addresses a particular concern or barrier you have in your practice at the moment, and a template is provided in Appendix 1.

- How easy is the tool to access and use?
- Do I need to register as a new user?
- Are there any limitations or restrictions that I need to know about before using it in my practice?
- Are there any special versions available for education practitioners?
- Would my learners be able to use it?
- How could I use it to enhance my practice: as a teaching tool; for learners to use independently or collaboratively; or as an assessment tool?
- Are there any network or security considerations I need to consider?

One of the biggest barriers many practitioners face when using technology in their learning environments are the restrictions and network permissions imposed by many security-conscious IT departments. We would always recommend trying out each technology in the learning environment you hope to use it in before trying to use it with learners. It is often worth communicating with the IT support department to ensure that the website you wish to use is not restricted.

These barriers are slowly being overcome as more and more institutions realize that overly restrictive settings and security protocols can have a significantly detrimental effect on learning. That said, many existing barriers can be reduced or removed with effective communication between teaching practitioners and IT support professionals.

Keeping connected

The tools and ideas identified provide a starting point for experimentation. There is a wide range of alternatives, with new tools becoming available all the time. Finding the space for this in our busy professional lives can be difficult, and we hope that this guide will provide an easy introduction to many of the popular technology tools that are being effectively used in education right now.

It is important to develop your networks and keep connected to ensure you do not miss out on the latest innovation which may enhance your practice. We encourage practitioners to harness the collaborative and social aspects of online technology to keep up to date, to share, to reflect and to participate in the ongoing conversation over technology and pedagogy.

1 Pecha Kucha

Pecha Kucha (Japanese for 'chit chat') is a radical slideware (such as PowerPoint or Keynote) presentation protocol conceived in 2003 by two Tokyo-based architects, Mark Dytham and Astrid Klein. They felt a need to come up with some way of helping designers speed up the process of showcasing their work to a public audience.

The 'Pecha Kucha' format ensures presentations are kept brief as the protocol allows only 20 slides, each delivered in just 20 seconds, creating a total presentation time of only six minutes 40 seconds. The slides advance automatically, so the presenter has to keep to the prescribed time. As a result, presenters are forced to rethink traditional presentation designs and delivery styles, using eye-catching and powerful visual images rather than large amounts of text in bullet points.

Pecha Kucha is a form of 'lightning talk' – short presentations, typically lasting around five minutes. Their aim is to engage with the audience, communicating key messages in a clear and concise way, and avoiding the much feared but all too frequently observed 'death by PowerPoint'!

Since its inception, the Pecha Kucha format has become popular with various professional communities around the world, with many artists, designers and architects holding 'Pecha Kucha nights' to present their work and latest designs. The business world has also been quick to adopt the protocol as a way of quickly presenting projects and pitches (see Klein Dytham Architecture 2011).

'Ignite', an alternative to Pecha Kucha, was launched in 2006 in the USA. Ignite events are now also held around the world to bring people together to share their passions. Many of these are themed around education and presented by academics and students. Ignite presentations are five minutes in length, following a protocol of 20 slides, with 15 seconds allowed for each slide.

How could I use it?

Adopting some of the principles of Pecha Kucha may provide a framework for reconsidering traditional presentation formats and content, in a bid to avoid information overload, boredom and ultimately 'death by PowerPoint'.

A Pecha Kucha presentation could be used in a variety of situations to stimulate interest and engagement, for example:

- to introduce a new unit, module or topic
- to consolidate or recap specific content
- as a revision tool.

You could also introduce Pecha Kucha as an assessment method with your learners. Ask them to create and deliver their own 6-minute 40-second presentation to demonstrate their knowledge and understanding of a particular topic or concept. Presentations could be recorded and used as evidence for summative assessment or as a self-assessment development tool for playback and critique. This activity may also be useful in developing and demonstrating learners' functional skills in ICT, as well as providing an opportunity to practise and develop confidence in their public speaking.

Where can I find it?

The Pecha Kucha format is a protocol for designing and delivering slideware presentations, such as those in Microsoft PowerPoint, or Keynote for Apple Mac users. Presenters should start with 20 blank slides and set the transition of slides to automatically advance every 20 seconds.

It may be useful to design a 'storyboard' of the presentation first to consider which images would be most appropriate to help communicate the presentation content. An example template is provided in Appendix 2.

'Impress' is a free version of slideware software available though Apache Open Office (www.openoffice.org).

For more information on Pecha Kucha:

Click: www.pecha-kucha.org

For more information on the Ignite presentation format:

Click: http://igniteshow.com

Anything I need to consider?

Although they last only a few minutes, the preparation time for constructing a Pecha Kucha or similar lightning talk presentation should not be underestimated. A storyboard structure may be a useful way to initially plan how the required content will be delivered within the time available. Scripting the accompanying dialogue may be necessary at first to ensure it keeps within the slide time allocation. Rehearsal and practice will probably be necessary at first to ensure delivery is punchy and to time. The use of a timer on each slide can be helpful to manage the delivery.

Images should be carefully considered to ensure they provide a useful and engaging backdrop to your speech. Many images available from the Web are under copyright restrictions, so care should be taken to ensure that appropriate permissions are sought and acknowledged. The use of images under the Creative Commons licence scheme can often be a good place to start:

Click: http://creativecommons.org

If using this format as an activity for learners to complete, less confident speakers may well feel anxious about having to meet the strict time restrictions imposed. For some, it may be more appropriate to record their narrative delivery over each slide, creating a short video or screencast recording rather than presenting 'live'.

Give it a go!

To start, consider one of your existing slideware presentations:

- How many slides does it consist of?
- How long does the presentation take to deliver?
- Is the delivery didactic and teacher-led?
- What are the key messages that you need to communicate?

Now consider an aspect of this existing presentation that might lend itself to the concise Pecha Kucha format. Would you use it at the start of a lesson to introduce a new topic, or as a recap perhaps? Could some or all of the presentation content be delivered in fewer slides and in less time? Would a shorter presentation give more time for discussion, activities and collaboration?

Use the storyboard template to outline the content on each of the 20 slides and the images that would feature. Use the notes section of the slideware program to add any text prompts that will help to remind you of the accompanying narration.

What are others doing?

I use the Pecha Kucha presentation format in a module called 'Sound Creation and Manipulation' on the BTEC National in Music Technology. My learners have to demonstrate they can use the editing functions of a synthesizer and sampler to build drum loops. Part 3 of their assessment is to demonstrate how they do that, so I decided to introduce Pecha Kucha to my department as an assessment method for the learners.

The other teachers were happy with the Pecha Kucha format and how it allowed learners to demonstrate their knowledge and understanding, particularly when attempting to gain the higher grades, such as merit and distinction. We have now written it into the BTEC assignment brief for that unit.

Presentations are short, but the learners really have to know what they are going to talk about and they can't read from the screen as they often used to do. As each presentation is exactly six minutes and 40 seconds, I can observe most of the group in one lesson. It also ensures they get a fair amount of time each, and they seem to really respond to the restrictions of the format.

Christopher – lecturer in music technology, further education college

I use a Pecha Kucha presentation at the start of each unit as a way to introduce a whole topic. I find it gets the learners really interested and they always ask lots of questions afterwards. It helps to set the scene and provides an overview of what they will be studying in more detail over the coming weeks and lessons. To help me keep to time, I sometimes rhyme what I want to say for each slide. This also helps to keep the learners interested and ensures I don't go over six minutes and 40 seconds!

Mark – lecturer in music technology, further education college

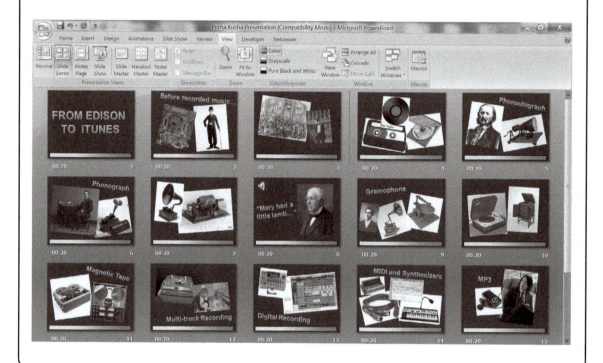

Reflection point

- Are there aspects of your current module or unit that would lend themselves to the Pecha Kucha format?
- Would you use this presentation protocol to introduce a new topic, as a revision or consolidation activity, or as a method of formative assessment?
- What are the disadvantages of the rapid paced format for you and your learners?

Finding and using copyright-free images

The effectiveness of very visual presentations like those in the Ignite or Pecha Kucha format rely on the selection of appropriate and engaging images to help convey the message to learners. Finding images online is often a quick and simple task, using internet images searches, but finding images which are free of copyright restrictions, even for educational use, can be challenging and often confusing. With potentially serious implications, the responsible and legal use of online images is an important consideration in developing our own digital wisdom and that of our learners.

The Creative Commons licensing system is one option for the busy practitioner to explore images with fewer restrictions. Many images on the social image-sharing site Flickr (www.flickr.com) are licensed for use under various Creative Commons agreements.

The digital media service from JISC provides a range of advice and support for practitioners in using the internet to find still images and video media in their teaching. A range of resources outline the complex world of copyright legislation and how to go about using your time productively to find the images you need.

An online interactive tutorial is also available to guide both practitioners and learners through the sourcing and use of images in their work:

Click: www.vtstutorials.ac.uk/tutorial/imagesearching

For more information on using digital media resources responsibly for teaching and learning, visit the JISC Digital Media service website:

Click: www.jiscdigitalmedia.ac.uk

2 Prezi

Launched in 2009, Prezi has quickly become a popular presentation format for users in industry and education alike. Prezi provides a 'zoomable' canvas, on which text and multimedia can be placed. The presenter is able to show the big picture and then zoom in to reveal specific detail. As well as a more novel and eye-catching way of presenting than many traditional slideware products, Prezi is useful for showing learners how different topics, aspects or concepts are linked together.

How could I use it?

Prezi can be used to outline specific topics, concepts and content just like a regular slideware presentation, although more uniquely it can be used to illustrate how different aspects of a specific topic are linked together and where relationships may exist.

The canvas approach promotes a visual representation of your information – rather than slides, Prezi uses frames where specific content can be displayed and grouped together in clusters. Information can be displayed in a linear format (like PowerPoint) or in a non-linear style. A strictly linear presentation which breaks down information into simple bullet points may be less useful for developing insights into more complex and networked narratives.

Prezi is a very visual medium, and the scalability of the software allows users to stress the relative importance of specific topics or terms. It is also easy to incorporate multimedia into your Prezi presentation, including online video. YouTube clips, for example, can be embedded quickly and you can choose at which stage in your presentation 'path' you would like to view them.

'Prezi Meeting' allows multiple users to collaborate in real time on the creation of a Prezi presentation. You might set your learners the task of creating their own Prezi on a specific topic for an assessment or to share with their peers. Using Prezi Meeting, learners can work in a collaborative online group from any location with an internet connection; they just need to access the link provided.

Where can I find it?

A free version of Prezi is available, although with limited functionality. Tutors and learners (with an educational email address) can use the 'Edu Enjoy' version, also for free, which includes additional storage and the ability to make your presentations private.

Click: http://prezi.com

Anything I need to consider?

If you are presenting in a location without access to the internet or the Prezi software, a portable Prezi is available; this however is not editable – so too late to make any changes!

Any online content, such as a YouTube clip will not work if you are using a portable Prezi in a location without online access. Be sure to consider your presentation location and its facilities.

With a free educational license, Prezis can be made public or private. Consider the content of your presentations and whether a publicly accessible Prezi is the most appropriate.

Give it a go!

Prezi has a function which allows you to import your existing slideware presentations (such as PowerPoint) in just a few clicks. Try this with a presentation you are due to deliver soon. Now consider how the functionality of the Prezi format will add value to this presentation, which would have been traditionally delivered in a very linear fashion.

- Would it be useful to rescale certain key terms?
- Are you better able to identify key relationships and connections between your content?
- Can you demonstrate how concepts might be grouped together?
- Does it help to see the 'big picture' in a visual way before exploring more detailed information?

Have a go at moving your content around and creating the presentation 'path'.

What are others doing?

I use a Prezi as the framework of a lesson. I find the software more dynamic and engaging and it helps learners to see visually how concepts link in a holistic way before focusing on specific parts. I have created almost 30 Prezi presentations on topics such as gender difference and social influences.

As well as displaying the learning objectives, I incorporate activities such as blank storyboards and spider diagrams that can be written and completed by learners when projected onto a whiteboard. I can also include YouTube or other video clips easily and they are seamlessly integrated into the presentation.

Numerous learners have commented on how impressive they think the software is! During feedback plenaries, I collect learner feedback on Post-it notes and regular comments include 'the Prezi used' or 'a different Prezi used' when the format has been changed for a new topic.

It can be very time-consuming, however, to create a really good Prezi. I usually download the portable version as the internet connection in class can sometimes be a little slow, which can cause it to lag during the presentation. It is also a good backup if the website is down. Sometimes the file size can be large, so it helps to create a zip file and have a large memory stick!

My Prezis are all available from the Prezi website, which means my learners can find them quickly and easily if they want to go over the content again in their own time. It also means I don't have to spend more time uploading them somewhere else.

It's certainly good for the wow factor and to reinvigorate sessions.

Samantha – psychology lecturer, sixth form college

Find out more

Prezi has an online education community, 'Prezi U', where members can swap their creations and discuss the educational benefits of this presentation medium.

Click: http://edu.prezi.com

Reflection point

- Do you have an existing PowerPoint presentation that might benefit from conversion to a Prezi?
- Which topics or concepts in your own subject area require a more holistic overview or recognition of the big picture?
- Are the relationships between concepts an important aspect of the understanding that learners need to demonstrate?
- Do you need any technical help to get you started on the Prezi interface? Can you identify a colleague who may have used it before and can give you some tips?

3   Social networking

The use of social networking platforms such as Facebook has taken the world by storm. Many of the world's most popular websites are examples of online social networks, where users connect to 'friends and follows' to share content, post comments, collaborate and interact. The accessible and intuitive interfaces allow users to connect to their online communities through their mobile devices, desktop computers and games consoles.

Messaging, media sharing and location tagging keep our friends and followers constantly updated on what we are doing, where we are and who we are with. This unprecedented popularity and ease of use by millions worldwide has led many practitioners to consider the educational benefits that social networking platforms can bring – but how can the principles of social networking be used for educational purposes in an effective and safe way?

Alternative open-source solutions allow tutors (and learners) to create their own secure social network environments focused on specific educational objectives, and can help to harness the benefits, and control some of the potential pitfalls, of these popular online tools.

How could I use it?

Tutors can take advantage of the interactive tools and features of social networking platforms, such as:

- posting questions for comments
- adding a poll for learners to vote on
- creating groups to manage classes, adding and tracking grades
- adding multimedia content such as video and hyperlinks
- organizing dates and events through online calendars
- sending notifications and receiving automatic updates.

Collaboration and communication skills are developed as users interact online to create and share content, as a group, whole class or whole institution.

Using a platform and interface that learners are comfortable and familiar with can increase motivation and productivity, as learning takes on an informal and social feel. The ability for tutors to easily communicate and connect with their learners to offer guidance, support and feedback is enhanced through the various updates and communication channels facilitated by a social networking platform. Learners can work together online to develop peer support strategies, making comments on questions, posts and uploading work. Grades can be tracked and discussion boards monitored for participation and demonstration of knowledge and understanding.

Where can I find it?

Edmodo is a secure social networking platform designed specifically for education and use with younger learners, but with the look and feel of popular sites.

Click: www.edmodo.com

Yammer is described as an enterprise social network and is designed for corporate organizations, but works well for developing social networks with adult learners and professional colleagues.

Click: www.yammer.com

Anything I need to consider?

The division between learning and living technologies is an area for consideration. Many learners are cautious of educationalists encroaching on their personal space and free time with educational content. Overuse may lead to 'social media fatigue' as it becomes a too pervasive medium.

The various privacy settings used with social networking sites can be complex, and it is important to explore the different information that can be displayed to the world. Concepts around security, data protection and online reputations should all be considered with learners as they develop their digital wisdom and online social responsibility for a digital age.

Most institutions and local authorities will have policies and procedures regarding the use of social networking sites by tutors and practitioners. The concept of 'adding friends' to social networking accounts blurs the boundaries of professional distance between tutors and learners if personal accounts are used. Set up a group or work account to ensure clear boundaries between social networking for living and for learning.

What are others doing?

I use Edmodo as a secure social network with my pupils. The kids love Edmodo because it looks like Facebook (I didn't think they would be that easily conned but they are!). I could message them about what we would be learning about and put links to resources ready for the lesson on Edmodo. I use it to post questions and encourage all the pupils to get involved in discussing what we have been learning online. I am able to help them learn about how to make appropriate and constructive comments that are focused on learning.

I loved the back channelling facility; for example, when pupils are watching a video as part of their learning they can comment on preset questions as they watch, or if I was teaching from the front they could message comments and questions as I spoke, making the learning much less passive.

Kim – English and humanities teacher, secondary school

4   Tools to create e-portfolios

What are they?

Electronic portfolios, or e-portfolios, are an increasingly popular resource for structuring, organizing and presenting learners' coursework and assessment evidence. The use of e-portfolios is increasing as teachers look for flexible ways for learners to create, store and manage their assessment evidence in a digital age.

Portfolios allow learners to demonstrate the product of their educational journey. E-portfolios also facilitate a recording of the learning process, as well as the product considered for summative assessment. A range of sophisticated and managed commercial options are available and adopted by many large institutions, although these may not always be the most appropriate option for the specific needs of your learners or sustainable financially in the long term.

A large range of open-source and Web 2.0 tools are available to develop different approaches to designing and structuring an e-portfolio. These can offer a number of adaptable tools that allow users to create, share, collaborate and present material for review and assessment.

Unlike a traditional paper-based portfolio, learners can easily upload and integrate multimedia evidence, such as video and audio material, in an e-portfolio. Hyperlinks can be made to other resources that are also online, for example blogs, online reflections, YouTube videos or online mind maps. This linked web of evidence can provide a rich demonstration of learners' knowledge, skills and understanding.

E-portfolios allow evidence to be structured, organized and mapped against specific topics, modules and assessment criteria. This can help learners to develop organizational skills and take control of their learning and track their progress and assessment.

How could I use them?

- E-portfolios can be used to support and assess a wide range of activities, such as individual or group projects, personal development planning, reflective practice or work experience.
- Many e-portfolios are able to provide a very structured framework for the presentation and organization of learner evidence, mapped against specific assessment criteria (for example those found in NVQs and BTEC qualifications). Hyperlinks can be added against specific criteria to view all the learner-produced evidence relevant to that assessment outcome.
- Web-based portfolios can be accessed anytime, anyplace through a login, enabling both learners and practitioners to use their time in a flexible and useful way. Learners can upload their evidence from home or on the move with their mobile devices. Practitioners can mark work from any location with an internet connection – no need to carry around large amounts of heavy portfolios!

- Coursework assessments often need to be subject to a process of internal standardization, verification or 'second marking'. Online evidence and feedback through an e-portfolio can mean this process is more effective, as verifiers and moderators are able to access work remotely and in a timely fashion.

Where can I find them?

A range of open-source options are being exploited on an institutional level, but often require technical knowledge and network access. Established in 2006, many colleges in particular are using an open-source e-portfolio product called Mahara, which integrates with the popular open-source virtual learning environment Moodle. Mahara offers learners a personalizable interface to upload and present their assessment evidence, as well as developing social connections and communicating with peers and tutors.

For individual practitioners looking for e-portfolio solutions from existing web tools, various applications available from Google are becoming an increasingly popular way of providing free and sustainable e-portfolio capabilities. A range of Google Apps are available, including:

- Google Sites: for the presentation of web content, including media-rich resources, as a linked portfolio of online evidence
- Google Calendar: for arranging, sharing and tracking events and appointments
- Google Talk: for online calls or for sending instant messages
- Google Drive: allows learners and practitioners to create, share and store documents, spreadsheets and presentations; Google Drive also facilitates real-time collaboration to allow multiple learners to work on creating documents together
- Google Groups: for creating manageable spaces to keep related documents, web content and other information in one place
- Google Video for education: for video hosting and sharing.

Google Apps are freely available for public use, or Google Apps for Education offers a free but more manageable and secure online educational environment. Many learners and practitioners may already be familiar with some of the Google applications from their social uses, leading to a short learning curve.

With no software to download, anytime, anyplace accessibility and the ubiquity and familiarity of the Google interface, many learners, practitioners and institutions are considering seriously the long-term sustainability of free web-based options.

Wikis (based on the Hawaiian word for 'fast' or 'quick') are online spaces where communities of users develop website content. One of the largest, most well-known examples is Wikipedia, an online encyclopedia of knowledge and information developed by its own users. Wikipedia is criticized in many academic circles as its accuracy can be called into question because anyone can edit and change the information – although this has also been its greatest strength in creating over 4 million free articles, for anyone, by anyone – a true example of constructive collaboration.

A range of free wiki sites allow tutors and learners to create online learning and sharing sites that can act as e-portfolios for sharing and presenting content.

Wikispaces

Wikispaces is a free and powerful online space for collaboration, research, communication and sharing. Sites can be set up for whole groups with student accounts for managing e-portfolios and assignment work.

Click: www.wikispaces.com

Other popular tools for the storage and presentation of information, material and resources include Dropbox and Evernote.

Dropbox

Dropbox is a file-hosting service, sometimes known as cloud computing, where users can upload their files for secure storage online. Dropbox synchronizes files so users can access, edit and upload their work from anywhere with an internet connection. Learners and tutors are able to share documents, such as assignments, with each other. Mobile apps are also available to upload and share evidence on the go.

Click: www.dropbox.com

Evernote

Launched in 2008, Evernote provides an information-management system that can be accessed through the website, or more commonly through applications on mobile devices. Users can store web content, make notes, record audio clips and store documents. Each 'note' can be shared with others, such as between learners and tutors.

Click: www.evernote.com

Evernote Peek is an application designed specifically for the iPad and its smartcover. Learners lift part of the cover to be presented with a question relating to their stored study notes, and can lift the cover further to reveal the answer.

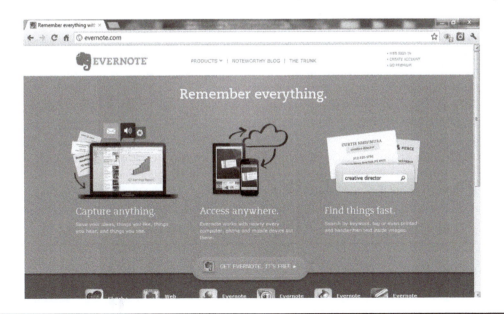

Anything I need to consider?

Many commercial e-portfolios require a significant financial commitment, and organizations will need to seriously consider whether this commitment is sustainable. Open-source or freely available alternatives often require significant technical skills, and technicians and development support, and in this respect also incur costs.

If using a combination of the user-friendly free web-based tools available, there may need to be a commitment to developing the skills of practitioners and learners in a systematic way, particularly if the e-portfolio is used for 'high-stakes' summative assessments which lead to the award of qualifications and certificates.

Many free services have data storage limits and these may not always be sufficient for courses where very large file sizes are required. Advertising is sometimes used to subsidize free tools and some adverts may not always be suitable for younger learners or vulnerable adults.

Using third party software applications may mean that availability and reliability become areas for consideration. If the provider were to withdraw their free services or if the sites suffered significant technical issues, how might this affect the assessment and evidence collection of your learners?

The assessment of evidence presented in an electronic format often demands a different approach to marking and feedback. Are you able to annotate the work as you might do by hand on a paper-based essay, for example? Are you able to upload audio or video feedback as well as written comments?

Different awarding organizations often have different requirements regarding the format and presentation of evidence for summative assessment for specific qualifications. It is always worth checking whether the e-portfolio system you are using lends itself easily to the formal assessment process.

Give it a go!

Click: Google Drive – www.google.com/drive

Spend a few minutes experimenting with Google Drive to see how quickly you can begin creating, sharing and collaborating with online documents:

- Create a Google account if you do not already have one – it is quick and free.
- Navigate to Google Drive and create a new document.
- Enter some text and share your document.
- Get the link and send it to a friend or colleague: they can use the link to collaborate on your document, add feedback or make suggestions.

Find out more

For more information on using Google Apps and other Web 2.0 tools as e-portfolios, explore the resources and work of Dr Helen Barrett.

Click: http://electronicportfolios.org/

What are others doing?

My learners kept on losing their assignment work or turning up to my class with very disorganized files and folders of the evidence they had been working hard on. I decided that an online portfolio was the way to go. By creating an e-portfolio with Google Sites, I was able to direct my learners to upload and save their work as soon as they had created it. They used a common template that I had designed, and shared their 'site' with me.

This was great because I was able to go into their e-portfolio sites and see what work they had created, and provide feedback on the quality of their work. It really helped me to keep track of how they were progressing, who was getting behind, and who was trying hard but not quite meeting the assessment evidence requirements.

It also helped them as they couldn't lose their work. They could no longer forget their portfolios and leave them at home as we could access them in any classroom with a computer and the internet. I was also able to use my time more effectively as I could dip in and out of their work whenever I had a few spare moments by a PC or on my iPad.

Setting up the template took the longest time, but it was really simple after I had experimented a bit. By getting the learners to use this template, it made sure that all the assessment criteria were covered and nothing was missed out. It also made it easier to mark and I didn't have a car boot full of portfolios to take home!

My learners upload files and documents, but some are now linking to more multimedia evidence, such as audio notes. I have found this provides great evidence for those who know what they want to say but struggle to get things down on paper. They are beginning to hit the higher grades as they can articulate their knowledge and understanding well verbally. I did check with the external moderator that this type of evidence was OK with the awarding body.

It has saved lots of paper too!

Linda – health and social care lecturer, further education college

Reflection point

- What are the advantages and disadvantages of using open-source and freely available Web 2.0 tools for creating e-portfolios?
- Can you identify a use for an e-portfolio in your current practice?
- How would your less technically able learners react to having to use an e-portfolio? Do you think the skills needed are a requirement for the digital age?

5   Blogging

What is it?

Blogs (short for weblogs) are basically websites where users can quickly and easily create written content to share with the world. Users add 'posts' to their developing blogs, which can be viewed and commented on. Blog narrative can be supplemented by a range of multimedia resources such as audio and video to make blogs more rich and interactive.

With the huge variety of free blogging sites available, anyone can become a global author in seconds, creating a huge potential for sharing information between study groups and individuals in diverse geographical locations. You can choose to follow your favourite bloggers and receive automated updates of their latest postings via RSS feeds or email reminders.

Find out more

RSS feeds

RSS stands for 'Really Simple Syndication'. An RSS feed is basically a web page which is read by a reader on your computer to stream the latest news from a specific website. RSS feeds are useful to keep up with the latest updates from specific organizations. Look for the orange RSS logo on your favourite sites.

Click: www.feedzilla.com

How could I use it?

- Encouraging your learners to get blogging can be a great way to develop literacy skills and encourage creative, factual or critical writing. The online written format can encourage many non-traditional learners to express themselves, creating tangible evidence for assessment.
- As most blogs can accept a variety of media formats, learners can find, create, add and share their writings, videos, audio recordings and podcasts, photos and more. This could be used as a simple e-portfolio for a specific topic or module.
- Blogging can be used to encourage reflective practice, perhaps during a group project, when creating an event or throughout a study process. By responding to other learners' posts, learners can enter a dialogue and demonstrate their critical reasoning skills.

- As a method of formative assessment, you can encourage your learners to critically evaluate your posts or links and explain how these are useful or not. Practitioners can monitor progress through blogs remotely, ensuring that contributions are being made on a regular basis.
- You could encourage learners to find their own favourite bloggers on a particular subject and to share these with their peers.
- Creating your own blog is a great way to share information, links and the latest subject-specific news to your blog followers.

Where can I find it?

There's a whole host of blogging providers out there, many with similar features and capabilities. More often than not the challenge is finding a provider whose design and interface you find comfortable and user-friendly. Examples of popular blogging sites include:

WordPress	www.wordpress.com	One of the more sophisticated blogging platforms out there, WordPress has a seemingly endless array of additional gadgets and add-ins for your blog.
Blogger	www.blogger.com	Blogger, from Google, is a very popular platform favoured for its ease of use and set-up.
Tumblr	www.tumblr.com	With its stylish and clear interface, Tumblr lends itself particularly to visual blogs featuring images and video content.
Posterous	www.posterous.com	Posterous, from Twitter, provides a very clear and simple user interface to post to your 'space'. Posts can be made via the Web, by app or by sending an email to your account.

Anything I need to consider?

Different blogs have different styles and features. It is important to explore some of the different platforms to find one which is right for you, your learners and the main objective of your blogging.

Blogs are traditionally public sites where users share their thoughts, comments and posts with the world. For education, it may be more appropriate to limit the audience. Some platforms allow private blogging to only those with a direct link, and others can incorporate a passcode so only those with the code can access them. Consider the content of your blog and who should have access.

The more sophisticated and complex blogging platforms may require more technical skills than the basic interfaces. Consider the skills levels of your learners when introducing the platform. Use confident learners to offer peer support to others who are getting used to blogging for the first time.

Many blogs are created each day and then quickly die away. They need regular 'feeding' and attention to attract readers and to keep them coming back and subscribing to your posting. Consider a collaborative blog, so there are more people to invest time in ensuring its success.

Give it a go!

Click: www.blogger.com
- Create a new Blogger account and give your first blog a distinctive name. Have a go at adding a simple post – just a few lines will do.
- View your blog and see your first post! Now make another post, but this time try adding an image or a hyperlink to a favourite website.
- Keep experimenting to see how each post adds to the next. You can quickly build up a number of useful posts to share your thoughts, ideas and information.
- See how your unique blog address is shared at the top of the screen in the web address (URL) bar. Share this with your colleagues or learners to get people engaging with your posts.

What are others doing?

I introduced the blogging site Tumblr to my Level 2 art and design students. They use the platform to provide ongoing updates on their projects. They can take images of their developing work and post these to their blogs, along with comments.

I have got into a habit of logging into my Tumblr dashboard each evening before class to see all the student blogs I am following. I can instantly see the progress they have recorded and this allows me to identify those needing extra support or more stretch and challenge. I record brief video and audio feedback and add these as comments to their specific pieces of work. Students are notified as soon as I have posted and it means they can receive feedback instantly, rather than waiting for the next session.

When we meet in class the next day, I am able to prioritize my support as the class continues with their projects. I can also work with the in-class support assistant to best direct their valuable support to their identified learners in the most effective way.

I encourage students to consider the privacy controls on their blogs and they can set password controls so only I can see what they have posted. The students like Tumblr particularly because they can really customize the user interface and express themselves, and the controls are really easy to use.

The blogging platform has really transformed the way I manage my teaching and the way my students manage their learning. I also created a course blog, where I can add links, images and assessment information; I find this allows me to model the use of blogs for students new to the process. Uploading documents and linking to other online content is so easy and it's a very accessible way of getting to the information quickly, rather than having to navigate all the way through a VLE.

Dan – lecturer in art and design, further education college

Having kept a regular blog for a few years before joining the course, I was already used to recording my thoughts and progress in this format.

I was really pleased when I heard that they were going to be using blogs to record our information. I find it a really clear way of making sure that everything we've been up to is there. As it is on the computer, I find that it is a lot quicker than writing everything down and I think it automatically encourages me to write more.

The other good fact about blogging is that it doesn't take any room. If I had been using sketchbooks I would be carrying round bulky paper, which would use up a lot of resources and probably encourage wastage. By blogging, it means that I can illustrate what I did with photographs, which I think is a great help for people reading the blog to get a better sense of my level of thinking.

Overall, I think blogging works really well for me and helps me to make better sense of the progress I'm making as I record it all down. I don't see it as a replacement for sketchbooks either. I could keep a sketchbook at the same time if I wanted. But blogging has definitely been the best way for me and I know that I would maybe not have recorded the course as well without it.

Bekah – Level 2 BTEC art and design student, further education college

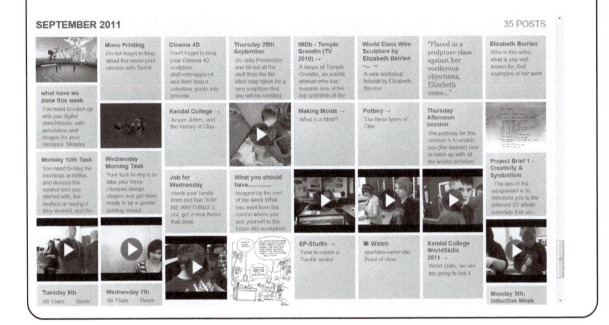

To investigate further how others 'blog', spend a few moments exploring two examples from the world of education and technology.

'Learning with 'e's' – the blog on all things digital from Associate Professor of Learning Technology, Steve Wheeler.

Click: http://steve-wheeler.blogspot.co.uk

'Don't waste your time' – the blog from Learning Technologist, David Hopkins, on e-learning, m-learning and all things in between.

Click: www.dontwasteyourtime.co.uk

Reflection point

- How might you use a blog in your own practice? Will you create your own blog to share and disseminate information or encourage your learners to create a blog themselves?
- Could you use a blogging platform as a way for learners to reflect on their progress and achievement or as a way of organizing and presenting their work for a specific topic or unit?

6 Phlogging (phone blogging)

What is it?

Phone blogging, or 'phlogging', is a similar concept to traditional blogging, but is a record of an author's thoughts and comments recorded by phone. Users submit their 'posts' by calling their phone blogging provider (or using a mobile app) and entering their unique code. Followers can listen in to posts via the website or a mobile app.

Many blog sites also allow you to make posts through your mobile phone or by calling a specific number and entering a code key for your specific blog.

How could I use it?

- Learners could be encouraged to create their own phlogs to practise and develop their speaking and communication skills, or to collect audio interviews for their coursework or homework.
- Learners on field trips, educational visits or taking part in events could use phlogging to report on their experiences or reflections. Other learners could listen in to be part of the experience.
- Practitioners could post their own phlogs to provide updates on a particular project or event where it is more convenient and practical to speak rather than type text. Learners can choose to follow your phonecast channel so they receive updates each time your make a new post.

Where can I find it?

ipadio is an example of a dedicated phone blogging site, where verbal posts are collected and shared. Phlogs on specific content could be created by practitioners for learners to listen to via their mobile devices, on the bus or train ride home from school or college.

Click: www.ipadio.com

Anything I need to consider?

Your phonecasts will be publicly available, so do consider the content of your phlogs and avoid any personal or sensitive information.

Ensure that your speech is audible and you communicate clearly. Keep your phlogs concise and easy to listen to.

Give it a go!

- Go to the ipadio website and listen to examples of other phloggers – see what they are talking about.
- Download the ipadio app to your smartphone device and experiment with creating your first practice phlog.
- Copy the ipadio player embed code and try inserting it into your own traditional blog or tweet the URL link to share with others.

What are others doing?

I encouraged my students to set up their own phonecasting channel to report on a community event that they were organizing as part of the unit on teamwork. Students are required to demonstrate effective collaboration and communication during the planning and implementation stages of their team activity.

Phlogging was a great way to record their updates and reflections during a busy event, where writing or typing information would have been difficult. Students also found it a fun activity and would pass the phone around their project teams so all could make a contribution.

It is worth getting your students to practise making a few phlogs first to get used to the format and so they do not worry so much about making a small mistake or 'saying the wrong thing'. After a few attempts their confidence greatly improved and I have found some are much better at recording their reflections verbally than on paper.

Greg – Access to Employment tutor, adult and community learning

7 Microblogging

Like traditional blogging, microblogging is a medium for broadcasting information to others via the internet. However, as the term suggests, microblogging is smaller, often with a very restricted word or character count.

Twitter, branded as a real-time information network, is arguably the most well known of the microblogging platforms, with well over 600 million registered accounts and over 100 million active users. Microposts, known as 'tweets', must not exceed 140 characters, although users can maximize the impact of their posts by incorporating weblinks, images and tags, known as 'hashtags' (#).

If you find someone is tweeting information you find interesting, you can follow them to receive regular updates of their posts. Users are also able to 'retweet' posts of interest to share with all their followers.

The increasingly popular use of microblogging by many celebrities has raised the profile of this particular technology. In March 2012, the *Independent* newspaper produced their own list of the UK 'Twitter Top 100', a ranking of the most influential users based on audience, authority and activity. The list included a plethora of journalists, entrepreneurs and celebrities, but how many educationalists? Only two academics made the list, but there are certainly a growing number of practitioners who are beginning to use the power of microblogging for teaching and learning.

How could I use it?

- The power of Twitter lies in building a community, a network of those you follow and who follow you. Receiving their concise words of wisdom and links to sources of online information can provide a targeted and specific resource stream.
- Like traditional blogging, practitioners can set up their own Twitter accounts to tweet and share comments, views, links and images with their learners who 'follow' their Twitter account.
- Learners can search for their own 'Twitter Top 10' in specific subject areas to receive a stream of updates from those in the know.
- By allocating a unique hashtag to a specific lecture or conference, practitioners can receive comments, questions and feedback from learners through tweets and backchannel communication.

Backchannel communication

Backchannelling is a parallel dialogue expressed through electronic communication methods by learners, or audience members, about an ongoing lecture or presentation. Learners can comment, question or provide feedback on a session by tweeting their posts using a unique hashtag code.

Practitioners can search for all posts containing this hashtag to collect all the relevant dialogue as it happens. Many are beginning to respond to these incoming comments, which can change the direction and content of the presentation as it happens.

Learners are able to pose questions or ask for clarification on challenging concepts as they are expressed. Practitioners can gauge the response of their audience and use 'reflection-in-action' to respond to demand where appropriate.

Different pieces of software can present this backchannel communication for all to see, with some practitioners building 'Twitter breaks' into their programmes. This instant two-way communication has the potential to radically change the traditional didactic transmission approach of many traditional lectures and presentations, highlighting the learner voice and its power to alter and shape the session outcomes.

Where can I find it?

Twitter – www.twitter.com is the most popular and well known of the microblogging platforms.
Visible Tweets – www.visibletweets.com and www.anothertweetonthewall.com provide attractive interfaces for capturing and displaying backchannel communication relating to a specific code or hashtag.

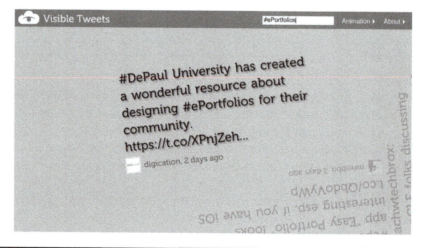

Anything I need to consider?

Communicating clearly and usefully in 140 characters or fewer can prove challenging at first, and learners may require some practice. This can help develop their literacy skills further.

Receiving a long list of 'tweets' from the people you follow can seem overwhelming and disjointed at first but this perception should change after some use. It can be useful to practise following just one or two people at first to get used to the format and the functions available. It may help to use an application which presents and organizes your incoming posts in a more user-friendly way, such as TweetDeck (www.tweetdeck.com).

When posting hyperlinks to other online content, Twitter makes use of the limited space available by displaying shortened URLs or web addresses. This can look unusual or confusing at first, but the link will work as usual. You can also shorten your own long URLs using sites such as TinyURL (tinyurl.com) or Google URL shortening (goo.gl) to maximize your space allocation.

When capturing tweets for display in a lecture or presentation, any post which uses the hashtag code will be displayed. This could include inappropriate or offensive messages, so caution may be needed. Commercial software is available to screen out unwanted content or it may be worth previewing tweets before displaying them, or blocking inappropriate users.

New Twitter accounts can attract a number of new followers that seem to be unrelated to your posts or interests. Many may be trying to solicit sales and marketing information; do not be afraid to block!

What are others doing?

I find the use of Twitter in my large lectures is a great way to engage learners and promote more interaction. I will pose questions at various points through the one-hour session, each with their own unique hashtag. Learners can then use their mobile devices and the university Wi-Fi access to send their responses. Tweets can also be used in a similar way to vote on a particular question or issue.

I use a PowerPoint template available from the internet (www.sapweb20.com/blog/powerpoint-twitter-tools) which captures all the comments on one slide in a user-friendly format. I can then review the responses to see where learners might be having problems or as a prompt for further discussion. It's a really useful way to get a quick idea of options from the whole room, and learners feel they are able to make a contribution, particularly those who are too introverted to speak out in a large lecture hall in front of their peers.

Not all learners have, or bring along, smartphones, laptops or tablets, but the minority that don't usually work with a partner who does. I have only had two mildly inappropriate tweets come up on screen since I have been using this method – but it has been a good opportunity to discuss appropriate use of social media and online reputations!

Pete – senior lecturer in initial teacher training, higher education

Top Tech Tweet

QRCodes! Easy to create, quick to scan, simple to share. Embed images, video or text. Try them as something different to enhance pupils learning.

David - Senior Lecturer in Teacher Education

Top Tech Tweet

The iPad is really useful for capturing video of dance techniques. These are uploaded to the VLE to show students what they need to learn'.

Peter - Lecturer in Contemporary Dance

Top Tech Tweet

Do you want to create unusual eye-catching presentations? Then get online and open a Prezi™ account. It's quick, easy and free.

Dawne - Senior Lecturer in Teacher Education

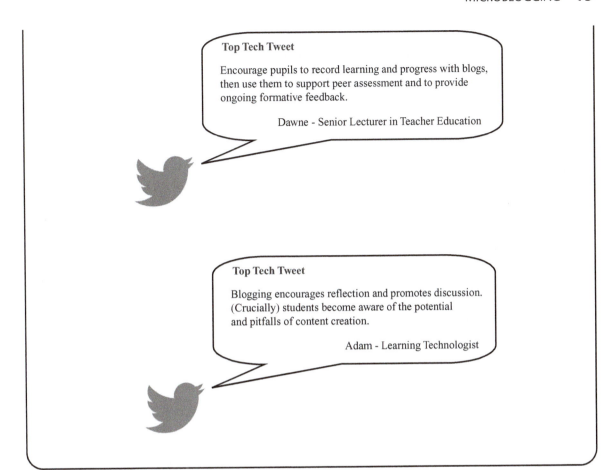

Find out more

EDUCAUSE provide a useful article on *7 Things You Should Know about Backchannel Communication* and its impact on learning.

    Click: http://net.educause.edu/ir/library/pdf/ELI7057.pdf

Reflection point

- Do you feel that traditional blogging or microblogging is a more appropriate platform for your own use in teaching and learning?
- How would you deal with incoming backchannel communication from your learners during a session? Would you respond to comments immediately, get back to individuals after the event, or explore trends and reflect on the impact for your subsequent sessions?

8　Inclusive technologies

What are they?

For some practitioners and tutors, the inclusion debate is often used as a barrier to the use of technology in the classroom. But many free software programmes and applications can now be used to break down the barriers to learning faced by many students with specific learning differences, such as dyslexia and dyscalculia, and physical disabilities:

- difficulties hearing, seeing and manipulating things
- restricted mobility and accessibility needs
- difficulties communicating and concentrating.

Inclusive technology tools can be used to empower learners to work with their specific needs to access learning in a way that is best for them. A range of tools can assist in this facilitation of learning, to promote independence and confidence, including:

- accessible user interfaces
- planning, memory and organizing tools
- writing and communicating tools.

How could I use them?

- Speech-to-text tools can be used to support learners who have difficulty writing or typing or who find they are able to express themselves better and more quickly through verbal communication. Speech-to-text software converts audio to written text to be used in assignments, for sending emails or to add to blog pages.
- Online curation tools and cloud storage can help learners to tag, store and organize their work and access it wherever they are through their mobile devices.
- Free online mind-mapping software can help learners to identify and express their ideas and organize their work into themes or topics.

Where can I find them?

The development of tablet computers and smartphones and their touch-screen capabilities has improved accessibility for many who are able to manipulate software through touch. A range of free apps are also providing essential tools for learners:

Dragon Dictate	A free app from the popular commercial providers of this effective speech-to-text software. Learners can speak into their mobile devices and the app converts the audio to text, to be copied, shared or emailed.
Image to Text	Take a picture of a sign, an instruction or a document and this app will convert it to text, which can be used with text-to-speech software to provide an audio commentary.

The accessibility features of many mainstream operating systems and office-based software, such as Microsoft Windows, have a host of tools and preferences to adapt to specific needs, including voice-recognition software, magnification and colour contrasts.

AccessApps

AccessApps provides a range of solutions to support writing, reading and planning, as well as sensory, cognitive and physical difficulties. Users can download a specific mix or all of the 60 software applications to a portable memory stick, to use on any computer at home, college or university.

MyStudyBar

MyStudyBar is a free downloadable application that combines a range of useful tools to help with planning, reading and writing, including text-to-speech software and mind-mapping tools.

Both AccessApps and MyStudyBar are available from the EduApps website.

Click: www.eduapps.org

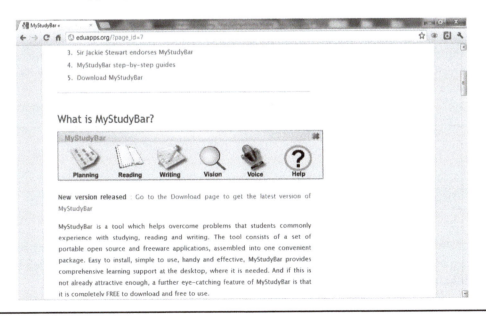

Anything I need to consider?

Learners' specific needs are individual and can be complex. A particular application of a piece of software may not be useful or appropriate for different learners. Additional learning support departments and specialists are often the best people to consult for more advice and guidance on how to support learners with particular needs.

Free products often have certain limitations or restrictions on them and may not be appropriate to meet a specific need – a full version or commercial software may be more appropriate.

Give it a go!

- Go to the EduApps website and download a copy of MyStudyBar to your computer desktop or a memory stick.
- Experiment with the different applications available.
- Consider how your learners might find the applications useful.

What are others doing?

We give all our students a memory stick during their first induction week at the college. It includes a copy of their student handbook but also the AccessApps software. This gives every single student a suite of free applications to assist with their studies. This way, the software is not seen as something 'special' or additional; it is a tool for everyone to use as they find helpful.

Jonathan – lecturer in additional learning support, sixth form

As a tutor, I find the apps available on the iPad really invaluable. I use image-to-text and text-to-speech tools regularly. I can take a picture of a document, convert it to text and then get my iPad to read the text back to me while I travel or do other things.

Dan – lecturer in art and design, further education college

Find out more

The TechDis service from JISC provides a range of information, support and tools for using both commercial and free tools with learners who would benefit from alternative strategies to support their learning.

Click: www.jisctechdis.ac.uk

9 Learner response systems

Didactic communication can be useful for the transmission of information from the tutor to large numbers of students, but it can be difficult to promote engagement with deep learning and understanding rather than just recall.

The use of learner response systems (LRS) encourages a dialogue between tutors and learners as feedback, questions and answers can be given in a two-way communication process. In smaller classrooms with fewer learners, this two-way communication is easily nurtured through sensitive and differentiated questioning, but in larger groups or with learners who are reticent about making verbal contributions, the use of technology to encourage audience response and interaction can enhance learning.

A range of commercial products is available to encourage learner interaction and dialogue but a number of web-based technologies are also presenting an alternative. Using mobile devices, laptops and netbooks connected to wireless internet connections, learners are able to interact with the learning experience, vote on topics, ask questions and give feedback to the tutor.

How could I use them?

- Response systems can encourage more introverted and less confident learners to make a contribution and to answer a question when they feel the answer may be wrong, promoting an inclusive learning environment.
- Tutors can pose questions or a debate topic and invite feedback from learners in a large lecture hall, instantly getting responses from the whole room.
- Collective expressions can be recorded and used as evidence for coursework and portfolios, or used as an initial assessment tool to find out what learners already know, to reflect and target the focus of the session.
- Tutors can ask questions to gauge understanding and find out when topics need further decoding and clarification, or to monitor the progress of individuals in a non-direct way.

Where can I find them?

Mentimeter is an easy to use response system requiring no downloads or technical ability. Simply pose your questions, select your options and get your response code. Learners vote online using the code provided and select their response. Tutors receive immediate feedback.

Click: www.mentimeter.com

Poll Everywhere allows up to 40 users to respond to each poll, for example answering questions, voting on a topic or expressing a view. Responses can be made via text, Twitter or through the website, using the response codes created. Tutors can receive updates immediately and respond or adapt their presentation as required.

Click: www.polleverywhere.com

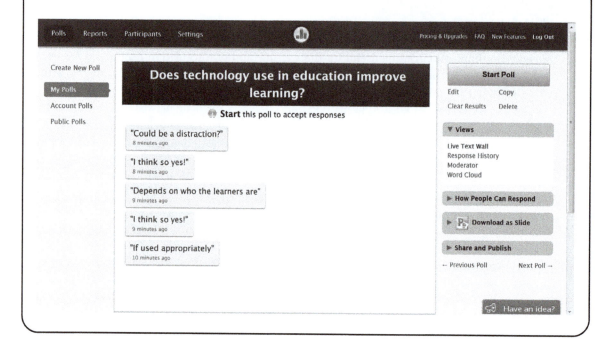

Anything I need to consider?

Users will need to participate via text message or the internet, so text credit or wireless internet access will be essential. Not all learners will want to use their text allowance on participating in a session, so this may be a barrier to some.

Free tools do not always allow the tutor to moderate the contributions made, so it is always worth reviewing the contributions first to avoid displaying embarrassing or inappropriate content on the screen to all learners.

Give it a go!

- Go to the Mentimeter website and enter your question and possible responses, and click start presenting.
- Go to http://vot.rs and enter the code of the question you have just created.
- Choose your answer and click submit – see how your vote is reflected on your question page.
- Encourage your colleagues to vote too!

What are others doing?

I use Poll Everywhere in my large lectures. I can have over 150 people attending and it is very difficult to manage two-way communications. As students are entering the theatre, I display a question for them to consider and answer. Many students use their mobile phone or iPad to vote and they see their comments coming up quickly on the screen – it's very motivational.

They are fascinated to see what others are saying too, so they are engaged right from the start. Occasionally there are some less serious comments, but nothing outrageous (yet!).

I also use another question or poll at the break to encourage feedback on the concepts they have been learning in the first half. This gives me an idea of what has gone in and what I might need to recap at the start of the second half. It makes the lecture less one-way and more interactive.

Carol – lecturer in initial teacher training, higher education

10 Wireless controllers

What are they?

Using the computer keyboard and mouse in classroom environments can restrict the tutor to the front of the room. Wireless devices allow you to control the computer, the mouse and the interactive whiteboard from around the whole learning space, so you can leave the confines of the main desk.

A range of commercial products are available which use a small USB device to communicate between peripherals and the computer. These can range from full-sized keyboards and gyroscopic mice (for use in the air) to simple mouse clickers and pointers. This equipment can be quite expensive, however, and the use of mobile devices and applications are providing new and innovative ways of controlling what is on the screen from around the room.

How could I use them?

- By using portable, wireless devices, the tutor can facilitate around the whole learning environment to check learning, to ask questions or to control behaviour.
- Learners with restricted mobility or low confidence can participate fully in activities without the need to come to the front of the class.
- Learners can use the devices from their own seats to take control of the computer and screen to make active contributions. This can save time as there is no need for students to get out of their seats and come to the front of the class.
- Learners could take it in turns to share ideas by typing into a document or online corkboard. Groups could work together on an electronic mind map and make their contributions before passing to the next. The whole group can observe as contributions are made and discussed.
- The wireless device takes the focus away from teacher-led activity to interactive and experiential learning experiences, which may engage the learners more.

Where can I find them?

Commercial products are available from a number of online providers and computer equipment specialists, for example: www.gyration.com

'Remote Mouse' is a free app available for Apple and Android mobile devices which turns your mobile phone or tablet into a set of wireless mouse and keyboard. By downloading the free software to your classroom PC, your devices can automatically connect to allow you or your learners to click and type from anywhere in the room.

Click: www.remotemouse.net

Anything I need to consider?

The range of any wireless device to the PC should be a consideration, particularly in large rooms or lecture theatres. Devices may become less responsive the further away you are.

If passing your tablet PC or smartphone around as a wireless keyboard and mouse, consider the possibility of accidents and breakages.

What are others doing?

I use my iPad and the remote mouse application as a wireless device to enable my learners to participate in starter activities. I pose a question as they enter the room on a virtual corkboard (I use http://corkboard.me). Learners take it in turn to pass the iPad around as they add a note and their answer to the board.

It's really interesting for engaging the learners as soon as they enter the room. As the different responses go up on screen, this stimulates a debate about who is right or wrong and generates great energy for the rest of the session.

Ben – Access to Higher Education tutor, adult and community learning

11 Digital curation

What is it?

As the amount of new information on the internet continues to increase, and social networks continue to expand, we are bombarded with a seemingly endless stream of data, updates and news. Finding the time to identify which information is valuable and worthy of our attention is becoming increasingly more difficult, particularly for learners developing their online research skills.

Digital curation is a term used to describe the presentation of online content which has been captured and presented for a specific purpose. Both tutor and learners can become curators, as they use Web 2.0 technologies to collect, organize, present and share useful information on a specific topic or theme.

How could I use it?

- Tutors can use a curation provider to collect and present information relevant to a specific module, concept, topic or unit. This can be shared with learners to direct or nudge them to explore appropriate and valuable information from reputable sources. Learners can spend more time reading, thinking and reflecting, rather than trawling online through the mire of information.
- Learners can be encouraged to become curators themselves, with a responsibility to collect valid and reliable news and views on a given topic. They can use the tools to creatively and attractively present the information for others, sharing with their peers.

Where can I find it?

A range of curation tools are available which collect, organize and present web content in attractive and accessible ways. Many have similar core features in terms of drawing together online information which can be shared, rated and commented on, although the design and presentation offered by each is radically different. Find the one you prefer:

Pinterest www.pinterest.com	A virtual pinboard to organize and share content. Comment, like and 're-pin' features for learners to select information for their own pinboard.
Pearltrees www.pearltrees.com	Pearltrees are created to group and manage websites of interest.
Paper.li www.paper.li	Create an online newspaper of relevant online content and share with others. Paper.li updates daily and draws on your favourite topics to update your information.
Scoop.it! www.scoop.it	Curate your own magazine of web content as favourite articles are organized and presented in a very user-friendly format.
MentorMob www.mentormob.com	Create 'playlists' of websites that highlight the most relevant content on a specific topic. Playlists are created and edited by the community of users.

Google Alerts are email updates of the latest relevant Google search results, based on a specific search term. You can choose how often to receive emails and what content Google needs to look for.

Google brings the information to you and then you can decide whether to share and publish the information using your chosen digital curation site.

Click: www.google.com/alerts

Anything I need to consider?

Curation of online information is becoming more important as the amount of data increases. The digital literacy skills of learners need to be developed to ensure they have the skills to navigate and utilize the range and scale of information to be successful in their education and beyond.

Introducing curation applications may start a discussion on how to be effective researchers online, how to judge and discriminate useful, valid and reliable information from the rest, and how to develop the digital wisdom to make those decisions to achieve their objectives.

What are others doing?

I encourage my learners to become digital curators themselves. At the start of term, we allocate topics for the specification to pairs of learners. Each pair takes responsibility for collecting and presenting online content that is useful for that topic. They are free to choose whichever programme they like, but they must share the link on the virtual learning environment and class blog.

It helps to work in pairs so they can share the work and discuss whether a specific resource makes the list or not! It is a great way to encourage the development of online research skills.

Every other lesson, a pair will briefly go through the new content that has been added. We show their online magazine or curated site on the interactive whiteboard and the learners talk it through.

Rajiv – geography teacher, sixth form college

12 Social bookmarking

Bookmarking is a process of saving the addresses of useful websites that you may wish to visit and use at a later date. Many people add these to their list of 'favourite' websites. Social bookmarking takes this concept a stage further, by adding the details of useful pages to an online list that can be accessed anywhere with an internet connection.

This in itself is very useful for the busy tutor, using a variety of personal computer equipment such as the home PC, the workstation in the classroom and the laptop in the staffroom. Social bookmarking lists can also be made available to other users, where relevant sites can be shared amongst learners, class groups or even year groups. This way, learners are able to access a list of peer-reviewed websites and online resources that will be useful for their studies and research.

Social bookmarking also makes the referencing and searching of sites very user-friendly. Each entry, or bookmark, can be 'tagged' with many useful descriptions to help categorize and highlight the benefits of each resource. Users can then search by using a combination of relevant terms and returning a list of pertinent resources.

We know that learners love to use the internet to search for information, but with an ever expanding Web of literally billions of web pages, it is becoming more and more difficult and time-consuming to filter, distil and identify useful information.

How could I use it?

- Tutors can signpost their learners to general social bookmarking sites to start their internet research. This allows learners to search a much smaller repository of information, which has already been through a peer-review process, and the chances of finding useful and relevant information is increased.
- Tutors could create their own bookmarking list specific to a particular unit or topic, which signposts learners to information they think relevant and academically suitable. This saves the need to print out or email learners with lists of websites that may change or move. Learners are able to access the list at any time from their computer or smartphone.
- Learners could be encouraged to create their own social bookmarking list, individually or as a group, as a directed task or assessment exercise. This creates a lasting resource to be used with future cohorts of learners.
- The use of 'visual social bookmarking' sites encourages more visual learners to access information relevant to their studies. If links are provided that need only a single click to access, this may encourage disengaged learners to engage with a wider range of reference material.

- Tutors could create an online 'treasure hunt' for information as a group or starter activity. Learners could be encouraged to enter the key 'tags' to find a specific resource or to find clues to the next link.
- Learners could take it in turns to add a link each week. Critical evaluation skills could also be developed as learners could be required to provide a justification for their choice and to explain how it is useful to their particular studies.

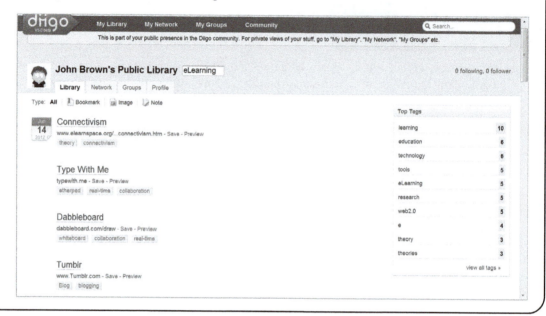

Where can I find it?

The range of social bookmarking sites is always developing, but some really useful sites to get you started include:

Delicious	www.delicious.com	One of the most popular and founder social bookmarking sites.
StumbleUpon	www.stumbleupon.com	Don't search – stumble! This site allows users to rate each site bookmarked and will match quality websites to the user's own preferences.
Diigo	www.diigo.com	Much more than a simple social bookmarking tool, Diigo enables users to select and annotate specific sections of a web page, add virtual sticky notes and share with others.
Only2Clicks	www.only2clicks.com	A more visual bookmarking site that allows users to create an overall view of favourite sites. Users can create tabs for specific reasons and keep these private or share them with others.

Anything I need to consider?

As with any peer-rated system, the information is only as good as the user who added it. Tags are a great way to reference websites but some users may add limited, ambiguous or inconsistent tags and make some information difficult to find.

Once on a social bookmarking site, it can be quite easy to get distracted by the other links available. While this 'digging' can be a really useful trail leading to similar useful sites of interest, some learners may get distracted or go completely off-topic.

Give it a go!

Click: www.only2clicks.com

- Access the Only2Clicks website and set up a free account.
- Start adding two or three links – these could be websites which you use frequently. Give the link a name and add the URL.
- Add some notes to your links, such as what the page is about or why it is useful.
- Click on your profile and give your Only2Clicks site a personalized URL. You can share selected links collections with your learners, for example for a specific unit or topic.

What are others doing?

My students were often asking for examples of useful websites where they could research further the topics we had covered in the lesson. I would add these to my PowerPoint slides so they could copy them down, but often they are quite long and it would take too much time for them to copy each character accurately.

Instead I used to email the whole group with the links I had recommended, but I wouldn't always have the time to do it straight after each lesson when some students had gone straight to the library to work on assessments and exam revision.

I had a mix of the most useful websites stored in my favourites list, some on my home computer and some on my work laptop. A colleague had told me about online bookmarking sites but it seemed too complicated.

As the number of links was increasing, I decided to explore the use of social bookmarking as a way to manage and share the links with my students in a timely way. I chose Delicious as I had heard of this before and it seemed to be a tried and tested site. You can add a button to your web browser toolbar and use this to automatically add the website you are visiting to your bookmarks.

I created a series of lists – or stacks, as Delicious calls them – for each unit of the AS and A2 syllabus. I can add my own notes about each site and what it is particularly useful for. I can then send an email invite to all learners in the group and also invite them to be collaborators.

Each week I choose a different student to add at least two relevant websites for the unit we are working on, to grow the list. They must justify their choice of site by writing how it is useful for their exam of the specification coverage. They have really surprised me by the choice of excellent resources – I have learned a lot too!

We can all make comments on each of the saved bookmarks – it really is a whole group list rather than mine now. It keeps growing and evolving and we can reorder the list as necessary. It really has been a useful process and it has certainly saved me time in the long run.

Martin – lecturer in information technology, further education college

13 Mobile learning (m-learning)

What is it?

'Mobile learning', or 'm-learning', is often used to describe learning that can take place when on the move, facilitated through mobile technology devices such as mobile phones, tablet computers, personal digital assistants (PDAs), laptops and netbooks, and even some handheld games consoles.

The pedagogical benefits of smartphones, tablet devices and the emerging 'phablets' are fast being explored by the educational community. As device ownership is increasing rapidly, many learners are now seemingly constantly attached to their sophisticated portable devices, accessing a range of multimedia tools and capabilities.

Smartphones – commonly referred to as mobile phones with a mobile computer operating system. They feature a range of more advanced features including high-speed internet accessibility, still and video cameras, digital music players, GPS navigation and touch-screen technology. Examples include the Apple iPhone and the Samsung Galaxy. The Apple iPod Touch (or iTouch) also has similar features to the iPhone, but without the telephone connectivity.

Tablets – tablet computers are portable devices larger than a smartphone but with many similar features, including touch-screen technology, on-screen keyboards, audio and video recording. Tasks such as browsing the internet, composing emails and working on documents is often easier given the larger screen size. Tablets often provide a very portable way to keep productive and connective, given their compact size, lightweight design and level of functionality. Many tablets also feature an accelerometer, which detects the physical movements of the device, allowing the screen to be used in many different directions. This flexibility is useful for resizing content in portrait or landscape format to best meet the needs of the user. Examples of tablet devices include the Apple iPad, Google Nexus 7, Microsoft Surface and the Blackberry Playbook.

Phablets – for those who find the smartphone too small and the tablet computer too big, a new generation of hybrid devices, so-called 'phablets', are also becoming popular. With a screen size between five and seven inches, the phablet is designed as the one device that meets both portability and functionality criteria. An example of a phablet is the Samsung Galaxy Note.

Laptops – along with their smaller cousins, netbooks, laptops are also regularly used to access and engage with learning on the move. Wirelessly enabled, and featuring keyboards, they lend themselves to sending emails, working on documents, browsing the Web and collaborating and interacting with Web 2.0 tools.

Games consoles – these include the Nintendo 3DS and Playstation Vita. They also offer touch-screen technology, cameras and online access as well as the gaming experience.

How could I use it?

These light and user-friendly devices are being used in many different ways by schools, colleges and universities. They have the ability to connect to wireless networks for learners to access a range of online materials and virtual learning environments, and use a variety of educational software applications (apps). The university lecture hall is regularly filled with learners accessing their tablet devices and netbooks to type notes, blogs and tweets.

Some schools and colleges are using class sets of tablet devices for learners to access online textbooks and handouts in PDF format. Learners can take and store class notes and conduct internet research.

Increased wireless internet (Wi-Fi) capabilities mean learning can take place both inside and outside the classroom. Many institutions are now able to offer complete Wi-Fi coverage in both public and study areas, with some libraries and learning centres offering tablet devices on loan.

Where can I find it?

Many institutions embraced the concept of the 'laptop trolley' to provide a flexible and portable way to transform standard classrooms into computer rooms, with personal computers for whole class groups. But significant issues with power charging, accessing wireless networks and security restrictions turned this empowering resource into a logistical nightmare.

The rise of more reliable and smaller tablet devices is giving practitioners a second opportunity to engage with whole-class use of technology to enhance and support their learning objectives. Portable tablet charging cases to accommodate multiple devices are being introduced to e-learning environments, giving practitioners and their learners access to a world of tools to support and enhance learning.

But not all institutions have the budgets required to purchase sophisticated equipment in large numbers. As the ownership and ubiquity of mobile devices increases, the value of the 'bring your own device' (BYOD) movement may offer many institutions wider opportunities for promoting mobile learning activities. BYOD anticipates and facilitates the use of the range of different devices that learners will bring to their schools, colleges and universities to stay connected and informed.

Practitioners who also embrace this cultural reality may find significant learning advantages in harnessing the power of learners' portable computers which they bring every day to their learning environment.

Anything I need to consider?

As explored in Chapter 1, concerns over the impact of the digital divide need to be considered seriously if learners without their own devices become disadvantaged. It is all too easy to assume that learners are returning to homes with broadband and wireless internet connections, and a variety of devices on which to access online resources and materials to support and extend their learning.

Although the use of consumer-based mobile devices is as natural to many learners as operating the TV, those who have not had the opportunity to use and experiment with them may have significant skills development needs to address. The time to become confident and familiar with any devices you plan to integrate into your practice should be a consideration built into schemes of work.

Some institutions are making significant savings through the use of freely available software and applications, and saving through changes to their traditional printing and administration processes. As such, many are reinvesting the money saved into the procurement of mobile devices for staff and students. Those able to provide equipment loans to learners need to consider legal and practical considerations, such as insurance and the use of devices for non-educationally-related activities.

A template for a home–school agreement for mobile device loans is included in Appendix 3.

 **Find out more**

A range of information and research publications are available on the value of m-learning and the impact on learning and learners.

JISC Mobile Learning infoKit provides a range of online documents, research publications and case studies on the use of mobile learning in education.

Click: https://mobilelearninginfokit.pbworks.com

Making Mobile Learning Work is a publication from ESCalate, designed for UK higher education, outlining a range of case studies showing how mobile learning has been used effectively, including the use of SMS texting for simulations and the use of handheld devices in initial teacher education.

Click: http://escalate.ac.uk/8250

What are others doing?

We have been running a project to explore the use and impact of iPod Touch devices on the literacy development of pupils. Each pupil is loaned a device to use at specific times in school and to extend their learning at home. This aspect was important as many of our pupils do not have internet access at home.

They use their devices to access the internet and the social networking platform Edmodo, contribute to their blogs and to read iBooks. Pupils access a variety of free iBooks and we read most days. This literacy intervention has been hugely successful, with measurable improvements in reading age but also a noticeable improvement in engagement with reading for pleasure.

Pupils have learned how to use the annotation facility in iBooks and the dictionary. I was also able to download free sample chapters which they could read and tell me the kinds of books they were interested in reading more of. They also use some apps for games-based learning and the voice recorder facility to capture their thoughts and to review books they have read.

The project has been running for two terms now and has had considerable benefits, particularly in developing pupils' literacy skills. However, there have also been a few technical problems with accessing some websites and cloud services in school. Some of the pupils also didn't have the technical skills we were expecting and needed initial support in using the devices.

Kim – English and humanities teacher, secondary school

14 Mobile applications (apps)

What are they?

Apps are a range of software applications that have been developed for use on mobile devices such as smartphones and tablet computers. A wide range of different applications are being developed every day, with over 200,000 available for the iPad alone. Each app is designed for a variety of uses, including education:

- business, administration and productivity
- music, news and entertainment
- sport, travel and lifestyle
- games and social networking.

How could I use them?

The range of uses for apps is almost as broad and diverse as the number of applications out there; however, they can be used for a number of different educational purposes:

- organization and administration
- researching and information seeking
- collaborating and sharing
- enquiry and knowledge gathering
- application and interaction.

Most of the major web-based tools also have applications which provide a user-friendly interface on mobile devices, for example Facebook, Twitter, Dropbox and Evernote.

Free applications allow multiple users to engage with and utilize the functionality of the software as an individual or a whole group or class.

Practitioners and learners could also experiment with building their very own apps to meet a specific brief or purpose. App Inventor (www.appinventor.mit.edu) from MIT allows you to develop applications for Android phones using a web browser and a connected phone. Learners could explore gaps in the current app market or develop app ideas to meet a client brief as part of a project.

Where can I find them?

This very much depends on the operating system of the mobile device that you are using. Most devices have a built-in link to access the relevant application download area.

- For Apple devices (such as the iPhone, iPod Touch and iPad) visit the App Store.
- For devices operating on the Android system, Google Play is the place to download apps.
- For Blackberry users, apps are available from Blackberry App World.
- Windows and Nokia device users can visit the Windows App Marketplace or the Nokia Store to download their apps.

Many apps are commercial products ranging in cost from less than £1 upwards. Many apps are also free, or developers offer a free 'lite' version of a particular app with restricted but useful functionality. Many apps have been reviewed by users, and this can offer a good insight into their overall use and value.

Some free apps to explore – download from your app store or explore the website first for more information:

Three Ring www.threering.com	Three Ring is an evidence management system app for tutors. It lets you create a digital record of your learners' work, from photographs, audio recordings and video clips. Enter the names of your students and use your mobile device to capture, store and organize their evidence in an online portfolio.
TeacherKit www.teacherkit.net	With the TeacherKit app, create your classes, add your learners and track their attendance, behaviour and grades. This mobile organizer also allows you to plot the seating plans of your students – great for the start of term or as a temporary tutor. Backup and export your data for analysis and reporting.
Paper from 53 www.fiftythree.com/paper	A very stylish way of creating online drawings and sketches in your virtual notebooks. Create your art or musings and then store or share them. Great for art, design or ideas generation.
Skitch www.skitch.com	Skitch is an annotation tool which allows you to add a variety of text, line and colour annotations to screenshots of web pages, maps and photos. Share via email or Twitter, or link to your Evernote account.
Audioboo www.audioboo.com	Create short audio recordings and share them with others as a link or as podcasts for followers to subscribe to. Audioboo provides a user-friendly interface for creating audio content to enrich e-portfolios, social networking sites and blogs.

Anything I need to consider?

Not all apps are available across all the different mobile operating systems, and this may restrict the use by some learners depending on their device. Many do have web-based options that can be accessed through a standard web browser on a regular computer.

Many free apps are possible because of the advertising revenue that they generate. The advertisements that are featured may not always be appropriate for younger users or vulnerable adults, so it is worth checking out.

The use of applications via touch-screen technology often requires a steady hand and fine motor control. For some learners, this may be challenging and not always appropriate.

Of course, not all learners will be able to 'bring their own device'. Practitioners should always be aware of the potential for a digital divide and have alternative strategies to address this.

Internet-enabled devices and mobile phones in an educational environment can be very distracting for some learners. The temptation to divert to other online content may be too great for some and cause disruption to learning. Be sure to check your organization's policy on mobile device use and how this should be managed. Outlining a negotiated acceptable use charter with your learners might be an appropriate activity to promote responsible device use and becoming independent digital citizens.

Your IT department may be using specialist software which allows tutors to control access to online resources or to control the screens of tablet computers – for example LanSchool (www.lanschool.com), which offers a free app for Apple iPad users with their commercial software.

Give it a go!

Educreations – Interactive Whiteboard app

Click: www.educreations.com

There are some great 'lesson'-creation apps freely available. They allow you to quickly and easily record video lessons for sharing with your learners. You can use the whiteboard feature, add audio, text and photos to create bite-sized learning objects which can be viewed again and again.

The functionality available will depend on the device you are using, although it is also available through a computer web browser if your portable device is not compatible.

1   Download the app for iPad through the Apple App Store.
2   Create your first video lesson by adding some simple text and recording your voice. Don't worry about what you say – this is just a test!
3   When completed, your lesson will be uploaded and made available for playback and sharing (if you choose).
4   Review your mini-lesson and try and share it by emailing the video link to yourself.

You could create a range of revision lessons and email or tweet the link to your learners to watch on their own mobile devices or desktop computers. Alternatively, why not get your learners to record their own video lessons as a formative assessment activity to demonstrate their understanding of a concept or activity?

Links to all videos could be collated and shared to create a whole-class set of mini-revision videos. A range of alternative apps is also available – which one works best for you?

Reflection point

- How might you use a whiteboard capture tool in your own practice?
- Can you identify a particular concept or topic that learners find challenging, where a small video resource would be useful?

Give it a go!

Nearpod – interactive mobile presentations

Click: www.nearpod.com

The Nearpod app allows tutors to create free interactive multimedia presentations that can be shared and viewed synchronously across up to 30 iPads or iPhones in one class. The tutor controls what is viewed on screen by all learners – this can include slides of information, video clips, and interactive activities and assessments. Learners work independently or collaboratively on the activities through their device and submit their responses.

Assessment results for each learner are available through the 'teacher app' to monitor progress and achievements and highlight individuals who may need additional support and guidance. Pace and content is controlled by the tutor.

1   Download the Nearpod 'teacher app' for your device.
2   Download the Nearpod 'student app' on another device.
3   Use the training presentation to see how the tutor controls the content on the learners' devices and how interactive assessments can be easily completed.
4   Go to www.nearpod.com to develop your own free mobile presentation.

Reflection point

- Is a tool like Nearpod something you might use in your practice?
- If your institution does not have access to class sets of mobile devices, are tools like Nearpod totally redundant?

15 Augmented reality

What is it?

In simple terms, augmented reality (AR) is an additional layer of information based on real-world objects and locations, accessed through mobile devices. Users view the real world through their application browsers and their phone or tablet's camera. Additional information is presented to enhance, or augment, this view – for example a video clip, animation or weblink.

AR is different to virtual reality, in that information is based on the real world. You still see the street, building, poster or person you are looking at, but additional information is provided on top.

The AR content can be triggered by a marker, such as an image or quick response (QR) code for example, or by location, using the global positioning system (GPS) of mobile devices. Content can be overlaid onto the visual trigger, for example a 3D model or video clip, or provide point-of-interest information about a specific location or attraction.

'Project Glass' by Google.

AR technology has been around for some time, and its use in museums and visitor attractions has been well developed. The use of AR in mainstream education has been a more recent focus of attention.

How could I use it?

- AR can be used in a number of ways to augment traditional materials. Worksheets and hand-outs can include visual triggers that AR applications will recognize and provide additional information – for example, a video clip to help explain complex or threshold concepts.
- Learners can use AR browsers on their smartphones to find out which building their class is in or how to get to student services.
- Complex concepts can be unpacked and scaffolded with additional content accessed through users' own devices – such as demonstrations and models on how to use a specific piece of equipment or how to carry out a procedure.
- AR data using location through GPS can be used for treasure hunts and quests as part of an induction.
- Learners and tutors can use free application software to develop their own AR content to enhance, enrich and augment their own materials to improve learning.
- A learner with specific needs or preferences may find learning more inclusive when presented in multimodal ways afforded by AR content.

Where can I find it?

A range of AR applications is available for different mobile operating platforms, including:

Aurasma www.aurasma.com	Aurasma is a browser to access location-based or trigger-based content through a mobile device. The Aurasma developer studio allows you to create your own AR content.
Wikitude www.wikitude.com	The Wikitude browser allows users to receive an additional layer of online information based on the location around them, including relevant social media updates and comments.
Stiktu www.stiktu.com	Stiktu is a fun introduction to the principles of AR and overlaying graphics onto real-world images, complete with social network sharing.

Anything I need to consider?

To access the augmented content, learners will need access to a mobile device, such as a smartphone or tablet computer, along with an appropriate app.

Much of the AR development has been in marketing and promotion, with education applications an exciting and ongoing development.

What are others doing?

In the plumbing department, we have developed a series of posters which are displayed around the workshop. They cover a range of topics, from simple plumbing techniques to how to use the different types of workshop machinery. This is really important from a health and safety perspective.

We give all students a comprehensive induction, but it can be a while after that before they use a specific machine. Having the poster there reminds them of what they need to be particularly careful about. The best thing is that each poster is a visual trigger for the augmented reality software.

Students download the app to their smartphone or tablet, and when they view the poster through the device the augmented content is displayed. We use an overlay which plays them a video of how to use the equipment safely. It takes them through the main techniques and how to stay safe.

The students absolutely love it. They really like the way the poster comes to life. It gives them the information they need to know, right when they need it. It has also made my life easier. I can spend more time on developing skills, rather than repeating the same information to 20 different students at different times.

Nick – lecturer in plumbing, further education college

For more information about unlocking the hidden curriculum with augmented reality, explore the University of Exeter's project report and blog.

Click: http://blogs.exeter.ac.uk/augmentedreality

16 QR codes

What are they?

QR or 'quick response' codes are a development of the standard barcode found on most commercial products. QR codes are two-dimensional codes that can be read through software and the camera found on many mobile phones, or through a webcam on a desktop computer. A code image can be scanned to reveal 'hidden' information, such as a weblink (URL), telephone number, social media profile or piece of text.

How could I use them?

QR codes allow learners to quickly scan and obtain 'just-in-time' information. There are many ways that these codes can be used for teaching and learning – for example:

- A code displayed on the last slide of your slideware presentation could feature a weblink directing learners to an online version of the slides for download from the virtual learning environment.
- Worksheets could feature codes with links to further information or with additional text to provide more explanation about a particular term.
- A code might link to an online social bookmarking list or Twitter profile, so learners can access other relevant pages or receive updates that are 'tweeted'.
- You might ask learners to create their own QR code for sharing with other learners in a 'code swap'. Learners take it in turns to scan each other's codes to find the information 'hidden' within – great as a revision activity or as a way to cover different aspects of a specification or module topic.
- QR codes could be used as an innovative and interesting icebreaker 'treasure hunt' activity. Working in teams, learners use a device to scan their first code, or clue, which provides directions to the next clue and so on. Learners work collaboratively to reach the end of the hunt quickly and claim their prize!

Where can I find it?

A variety of free QR code generators are readily available online and can be found with a simple search using a well-known search engine, such as Google. Some examples include:

- **QR Stuff**: www.qrstuff.com
- **Kaywa**: http://qrcode.kaywa.com
- **University of Bath**: www.bath.ac.uk/barcodes/create

Users will also need a QR code reader, or scanner. Smartphones and tablet devices may already have the necessary software installed or a variety of free 'apps' are available, including:

- **Neoreader**: www.neoreader.com – to install the reader onto a mobile device, users should go to: get.neoreader.com
- **BeeTagg**: www.beetagg.com

Desktop computer users can also access data in QR codes by using a webcam or screen capture. Quickmark (www.quickmark.com) provides free software that will allow you to read QR codes from websites, PDF documents or accessed through a connected webcam.

Anything I need to consider?

Not all learners will have ready access to mobile devices with cameras and QR code-scanning software. However, smartphone ownership is increasing rapidly and desktop readers are available for desktop PCs and laptops.

Not all software is compatible with every mobile device, and it is useful to check whether the application will work with less popular devices.

Give it a go!

Download your QR code reader and try scanning the following examples of QR codes to find the hidden data.

This is an example of a code containing text. This could be used to provide further information on a complex topic, or to provide a list of references used in a presentation, perhaps.

This is an example of a code containing a link to a web page or URL. If users are connected to the internet through their device, they can go straight to the identified page. This could be a link to a Twitter account, RSS feed, blog, YouTube clip or social bookmarking list, for example.

This is an example of a code containing data to send a text (SMS) message. This saves time entering a phone number and typing text and could be used with SMS voting, for example.

This is an example of a code containing location details which will identify a specific destination on a map. This could be used during an induction to highlight where a specific building is on a large campus.

This code provides contact details. They could include your office telephone number or work email address or the contact details of the student support department. Learners could be encouraged to scan the code and save the details into their phones for future use.

What are others doing?

As a private training provider, I move around the country on a regular basis and meet many different trainees and learners. I am often asked for my telephone number, email address, Twitter profile name, LinkedIn profile – the list is getting longer as different people want to connect with you in their preferred way.

I have started to use a Kimtag (www.kimtag.com), which generates a QR code. My learners and contacts can scan the code on their smartphones and it gives them a menu of methods to get in contact. It has saved me time and it also ensures they get the right details. It is getting more difficult to remember all my different usernames and profiles!

Allan – independent professional trainer

The University of Bath have completed various projects on the use of QR codes in higher education. You might find their QR blog a useful source of further information and ideas.

Click: http://blogs.bath.ac.uk/qrcode

17 Screencasting

What is it?

Just as pressing the 'PrtScrn' print screen button on your keyboard takes a shot of everything visible at that time on your computer screen, screencasting software allows users to capture a video recording of on-screen activity. Images can be supplemented with audio narration to talk through the activity taking place.

How could I use it?

Capturing on-screen activity can have a number of different uses:

- You could 'flip' a traditional teaching approach by recording a brief lecture or lesson featuring your presentation slides, weblinks and audio narration and allow learners to engage with this transmission content in their own time. This would leave supervised in-class time for discussion, debate and more active learning experiences.
- As part of a course or college induction, a video clip could be produced to demonstrate how learners might use part of the VLE, the student information system, or an electronic portfolio.
- Video tutorials or feedback could be captured for playback at a later time to check what was discussed or to reflect on actions agreed.
- Online assignment briefs or tasks could be enhanced with short clips providing a multimedia interpretation of what is required, to demystify expectations or make materials more inclusive for those with specific needs.
- Learners could produce their own screencasts as a form of assessment to demonstrate their understanding of a piece of software, to evaluate a specific website or show the sequential procedures required in a particular online task.

Screencasts can be stored online for sharing and playback. They could be integrated into blogs, social networking sites or areas of a VLE which are course- or subject-specific.

Where can I find it?

A range of simple, free web-based screen-recording tools are available, alongside more sophisticated commercial products. Some free web-based examples include:

- Screenr: www.screenr.com
- Screencastomatic: www.screencast-o-matic.com
- Screencast.com: www.screencast.com

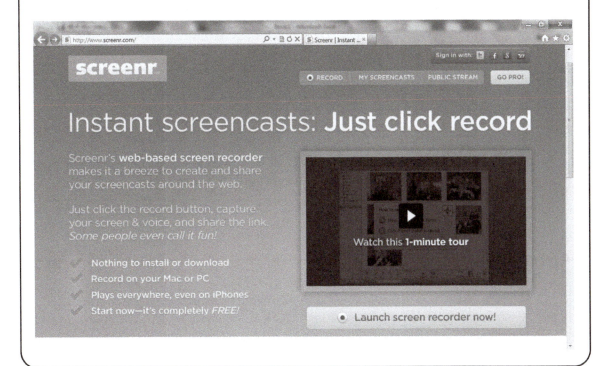

Anything I need to consider?

Some screencasting software places a limitation on the length of the video you can record. This should not be too prohibitive, and helps to keep clips concise, user-friendly and of a manageable size.

Consider the audience for your video and whether you need software which ensures your screencast is kept private or password protected. Also consider where your screencast is likely to be played back. If you are capturing small images or text, this might be very difficult to see when played back on a smartphone screen.

Communicate clearly. Choose a good-quality microphone to help ensure your audio narration is clear. Practise what you wish to say before pressing the record button or have a script of bullet points to ensure your narration is smooth.

Be careful with data protection. Choose what you want to capture bearing in mind that some software captures everything on the screen. Have you closed unnecessary windows and browsers? Are you capturing sensitive or personal information in your screencast?

Screencasting software may use third party applications such as Java and Flash. If your computer does not have the latest versions of these free downloads, they may need to be updated. Sometimes download restrictions on computers in schools, colleges and universities require an administrator to allow these updates. Contact your IT support office if you encounter these small initial barriers.

Give it a go!

- Go to www.screenr.com and click the record button.
- Resize the frame over an open browser displaying a website of your choice. Ensure your microphone is connected (if appropriate).
- Press record and explain the various features of the website chosen, and click through a few links. When completed, press 'done' and publish your screencast.

Reflection point

- How could you use screencasting as a formative assessment tool for your learners?
- Consider how you might best share the videos you create with your learners – in a blog, through the VLE or via the Screenr site?
- How might you use a screencast with learners before their induction to introduce them to your institution or course before they arrive?

What are others doing?

I used screencast-o-matic with my information technology and computing students. As they complete their coursework tasks in programming and website authoring, they are able to create small video clips on their progress or to outline a specific issue they are having.

Learners share their screencast links with me for playback and feedback. I can access the clips via my tablet or smartphone when travelling or away from the classroom. I can provide written feedback via email, or I am able to create my own screencasts to demonstrate visually how to complete a specific software task or to provide further prompts for reflection. This gives me more time in class to spend on introducing new topics or supporting those learners who need face-to-face guidance.

I have found that some of the more introverted learners are sometimes more comfortable with creating a screencast than raising a problem or issue in front of others. The record of screencasts also helps when we come to review and measure progress. It is clear to see the distance travelled and check understanding of areas that have proved challenging.

Martin – lecturer in information technology, further education college

What is the 'flipped classroom'?

The flipped classroom is a pedagogical approach that reprioritizes the sometimes traditional role of the lecturer. Rather than spending the session time delivering a lecture to a whole group of learners, the knowledge-transmission role traditionally undertaken by the practitioner is replaced by a video, featuring presentation visuals (such as slides) and audio narration. Screencasting software can be used to create this multimedia resource. An online assessment or quiz is also used to instantly gauge the learners' grasp of the content.

Learners engage with the resources in their own time through their computers or mobile devices and then spend the session engaged in more experiential, collaborative and interactive activities. The tutor becomes the facilitator of learning, the 'guide on the side', rather than the transmitter of knowledge, or the 'sage on the stage'.

This approach assumes a very traditional, behaviourist approach to lecturing and does not take into account the more interactive approaches to delivery of content to whole groups, such as discussion and questioning. It also raises questions around the quality of instruction and how to best facilitate a group of learners, many with different needs. It does, however, highlight an interesting consideration over the use of screencasting and automatic online assessments and their role in allowing practitioners to focus on more constructivist pedagogies.

Find out more

Educational association EDUCAUSE have produced a guide featuring *7 Things You Should Know about Flipped Classrooms*.

Click: http://net.educause.edu/ir/library/pdf/ELI7081.pdf

18 Serious games

Games can be played on personal computers, handheld devices or consoles, and online with thousands of others simultaneously, sometimes known as massively multiplayer online (MMO). The more recent developments in the range of highly interactive and participatory computer- and console-based games market offer a range of opportunities for practitioners to harness the appeal of these technologies with learners, to reinforce learning in an informal and accessible way.

Serious games is the term often used for games which have a primary learning focus, rather than just entertainment, although these games can also develop many skills and competencies desirable for a digital age, such as problem solving and critical thinking.

Games-based learning (GBL) using devices such as the Nintendo Wii and Microsoft Kinect provide a very kinaesthetic way for users to interact with online material. The way that games motivate performance with reward raises interesting considerations for strategies to promote engagement as well as online collaboration.

Games are often a favoured pastime for many learners and can be powerful in motivating and engaging learners disengaged from traditional learning activities, promoting a sense of determination and desire to succeed.

The impact of games-based learning is also being explored by neuroscience researchers, looking at the impact of interaction on the brain and our abilities to make quick decisions about the outcome of actions.

How could I use them?

- Games can promote the skills of critical thinking, decision making and problem solving as learners take responsibility for their own progression and achievement in a games environment.
- Learners can self-assess their progress as they participate in active learning and receive feedback. Games often adapt to the individual's level of performance to provide optimal challenge.
- Multi-user games can promote the development of collaboration and teamwork.
- Games can develop subject-specific skills such as science, literacy, maths and engineering through problem-based learning and scenarios.
- Reflection practice can also be developed as learners consider their decisions and the consequences of their actions.

- An inclusive classroom could be enhanced with such technology for learners whose fine motor control is problematic, or to explore and develop emotional responses and reactions to different stimuli.
- The interactive whiteboard takes on a different level of engagement as users are able to use gestures and movement to interact and respond, for example in a dance class or when practising techniques that involve particular movement and control.
- Some learners might be able to create their own games as a way of demonstrating their skills in programming and design for other learners to engage and interact with.

Where can I find them?

Scratch, developed by the MIT Media Lab, is a programming language that makes it easy to create interactive games which can be shared on the Web.

Click: www.scratch.mit.edu

Also designed for children and young people, Kodu is a simple visual programming language that lets any user easily create visual games on a PC or via an Xbox games system, without any previous programming experience.

Click: http://fuse.microsoft.com/page/kodu

Anything I need to consider?

The use of games for learning purposes further blurs the traditional boundaries of living and learning, as well as formal and informal learning. Many learners are highly motivated by games but others are not.

The learning objectives of using games should be carefully considered so they are used in an appropriate way to enhance the outcomes for learners, whether this be skills development, motivation and engagement or reward.

Games used by learners at home may not always be appropriate for the classroom. Many feature violent and sexual themes and have recommended age restrictions. Indeed, there are various criticisms of computer games more generally, including the promotion of violence, social isolation and the impact on health and well-being. The choice of games for learning should avoid reinforcing these concerns but focus on developing the engagement of learners and extending learning opportunities.

When using any visual media, regular breaks must be scheduled to prevent fatigue and issues around ergonomics and posture. This can sometimes be difficult when learners become very engaged in achieving a particular level or goal.

Give it a go!

Click: www.stopdisastersgame.org

Explore an example of an online simulation game, 'Stop Disasters', from the United Nations and the International Strategy for Disaster Reduction, where players attempt to stop disasters from occurring by building defences. Players develop strategies and skills to build resources, within their budget and time frame, to reduce the impact of a range of natural disasters.

What are others doing?

In my citizenship class, pupils use the online simulation games from Channel 4 learning (www.channel4learning.com/sites/lifestuff). They cover a range of topics, including racism and bullying, sexual health, politics and the economy. The interactive games are a great way to break up the lesson and consolidate learning as pupils work in pairs to answer the questions and move through the levels.

They can get quite competitive and it can be really motivating for some. I find they stay on task really well, although the laptops are not always available and I have to make sure I book them well in advance.

Claire – religious studies and citizenship teacher, secondary school

 **Find out more**

A report by Futurelab on *Games-Based Experiences for Learning* provides a useful overview of what makes a digital game a motivating and engaging learning experience, as well as a set of design principles for digital games-based learning experiences.

Click: www.futurelab.org.uk/resources/games-based-experiences-learning

Engage (European Network for Growing Activity in Game-based learning in Education) is a central information resource for people interested in games for learning and using games for curricular contents.

Click: www.engagelearning.eu

19 Online creative collaboration tools

Tutors often promote collaboration and group work in their classes as a way of developing deeper learning. Outside of the learning environment, it can be more difficult for learners to work together on projects and tasks, especially if they live far apart.

A number of Web 2.0 tools promote real-time synchronous collaboration in creative ways, including mind-mapping, brainstorming and ideas-harvesting. By working together online, learners can extend the benefits of group and teamwork to produce learning objects which demonstrate knowledge and understanding.

Online collaboration at its best: the wiki is an easy way for learners to create a collaborative piece of evidence. The use of 'real-time', online wikis can create an engaging and dynamic creative environment, where learners can shape ideas, concepts and evidence.

How could I use them?

- Learners can work together on a group mind map to identify ideas for a new topic, project or task. They can explore team roles, deadlines and project plans by collaborating, discussing and negotiating in real time from any location with an internet connection.
- Mind maps help to identify links and relationships, priorities, and the scope of a given topic, for further research.
- Online notepads and whiteboards provide a blank space for learners to generate and discuss ideas before refining them down into concrete concepts. They are great tools for new teams and groups to use to explore project ideas.
- Learners in rural locations can connect online with their peers to continue teamwork started in the classroom or seminar group. Work is stored and saved online, and learners are able to review the history and go back to previous versions for review and reflection.
- Team leaders and moderators can take control by using 'presenter' functions to lead discussions on collaborative pieces – developing leadership, communication and emotional intelligence skills.

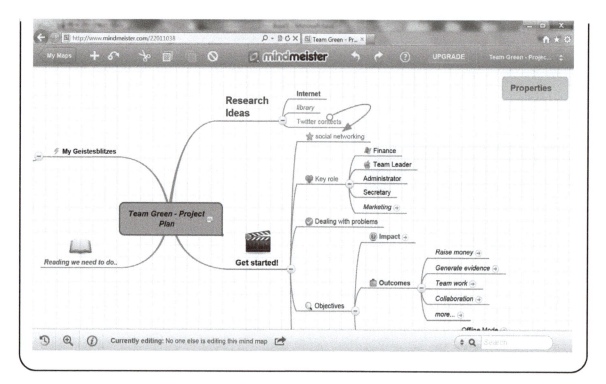

Where can I find them?

A range of online collaborative tools is freely available over the internet. Google Drive (www.google.com/drive – previously Google Docs) also has a range of collaborative functions for working on documents together.

MindMeister www.mindmeister.com	Online brainstorming and mind-mapping software. Up to 30 users can collaborate at once on a single map. Maps can be published and presented on blogs and websites. A presentation mode is available to allow the moderator to control the map for presentation and review.
TypeWithMe www.typewith.me	An online notepad for real-time collaborative writing. Work on the same document together at the same time from any location. Use the unique URL code to access the same 'pad'. Individual contributions can also be tracked.
PBworks www.pbworks.com	An online collaborative wiki (Hawaiian for 'quick'!) provides a space for teams and groups to collaborate, share files and organize projects. Updates are tracked, so you can see what has changed and who has been contributing.
Popplet www.popplet.com	Popplet is a visual board for recording thoughts and images. Groups can collaborate in real time to create and share their ideas. Each idea or image 'popplet' can be arranged into a presentation for display.
Wallwisher www.wallwisher.com	An online noticeboard for collaborative brainstorming and ideas sharing. Users can post sticky notes, and add links and images to generate their idea. Invite others or give them the unique URL code to join your board.

Anything I need to consider?

Many of the free sites display creations publicly, so consider what information is being shared if there is no option for a private account.

Not all members of a group or team are guaranteed to have internet access outside school, college or university, so consider the impact of using online collaborative tools for those that might be disadvantaged.

As the tools are online, groups can give tutors access to review contributions and give feedback. Encourage learners to share their online space links with you to review their contributions. It is useful if individuals label their own contributions, so you can see who is engaging in the group process and who might need more support.

What are others doing?

I encourage students to use an online notepad (like www.piratepad.net) to work together when generating ideas for their coursework. This actually is part of their assessment criteria, so producing a product that can be shared and printed as evidence is really useful.

The fact that you can review the history of a map is also good, in case you need to go back to earlier ideas or those that were deleted. When using collaborative work as evidence for coursework and summative assessment, it is really important to make it clear who has made what contribution. I love the fact that a collaborative notepad colour-codes individual contributions. This makes it really obvious who has done what and I can take this into consideration when marking.

Andy – lecturer in sport, further education college

20 Digital storytelling

What is it?

A picture paints a thousand words and digital books and photo storyboards can be a really useful assessment method for learners to express their knowledge and understanding of a particular topic or subject.

Digital storytelling uses computer tools to create engaging resources which tell a story, most commonly as a video resource, but also as an online book or multimedia presentation. Designing and creating digital stories can engage, motivate and inspire learners, whilst developing communication, creativity and literacy skills.

Stories can be personal, fictional or factual. They can be used to facilitate rich self-reflection or to develop social and cultural awareness and understanding.

How can I use it?

- Using copyright-free or original photos and images, learners can individually or collaboratively create a story, combining visual images with annotations, music and narrative to explain, discuss or evaluate.
- Storyboards can be shared or embedded in virtual learning environments, blogs and web pages. Group storytelling encourages teamwork, negotiation and creativity. It can promote multimodal literacy development and expression.
- Tutors can create their own engaging and emotive photo storyboards to introduce a new topic, stimulate debate, or as a break between sessions. The mix of audio, images and text can create a powerful visual resource that inspires and captivates learners.

Where can I find it?

Click: www.animoto.com

Animoto provides a very simple interface to easily and quickly create professional looking presentations which combine music, video clips, images and text. Tutors can access a free Educators account for use in the classroom. Presentations can be shared and embedded into blogs and social networking sites to add more engaging elements.

Click: www.storybird.com

Not a video platform, Storybird allows users to create illustrated digital storybooks in a few simple clicks. Starting with a library of colourful illustrations, the story is designed around the images rather than illustrations being chosen to support the text. Designed for younger readers, Storybird is a useful resource for promoting creativity – for example, for trainee primary school teachers looking to create resources for and with their learners.

Click: www.storify.com

Storify allows users to create rich narratives supported by social media elements. For example, learners could create a personal reflective piece, using images drawn from their Facebook account, posts they have sent and received on Twitter, YouTube clips, or other web content. Their Storify can be saved and published for sharing back to their online social media outlets.

Anything I need to consider?

Different digital storytelling software comes with its own library of soundtracks and illustrations. When using other material, due consideration of copyright restrictions should be given to material taken from other online sources.

Learners should be encouraged to plan their stories in advance, using storyboard techniques to structure and design their approach before production.

Digital stories are usually quite short, lasting around three to ten minutes, although production time can be considerable, especially if original media is used. This should be built into the scheme of work or lesson plan if used as a directed activity.

Give it a go!

- Go to the Animoto website and sign up for a free account.
- Choose a style for your first video and experiment with adding some text and images.
- Publish your story and playback.

What are others doing?

I used Animoto to create an introductory presentation on the origins of World War II and Nazi Germany. The blend of music, images and video clips created a powerful five-minute introduction to the unit.

I asked learners to discuss and identify what they already knew about the topic following the presentation. I also set a formative assessment task in groups, where learners had to interview relatives or neighbours about what life was like in post-war Britain. They could take images of any old artefacts and audio or video recordings (with permission) of their interviewees.

Learners found the software really easy to use and some of the results were very professional. They enjoyed creating a product as evidence of their research and sharing it with their peers. I know that some were very proud to show their digital stories back to their grandparents. I think it really helped them to gain a deeper understanding of the impact of the war from a personal perspective.

Rebecca – history teacher, sixth form college

The Center for Digital Storytelling provides a useful overview of the main principles and benefits of storytelling through digital methods, with case study examples from education providers.

Click: www.storycenter.org/education

Catherine Boase from the University of Gloucestershire presents a study of the uses and potential of digital storytelling for reflection and engagement.

Click: http://tinyurl.com/digital-storytelling-use

21 Avatars and virtual characters

Online materials can be dull and uninspiring, particularly for the 14–19-year-old learner experienced in all things interactive! The use of avatars – or virtual characters – can be a novel way of bringing online materials to life and of developing creativity.

An avatar is basically a graphical representation of a human character. You can create avatars which represent you, or someone completely different. Avatars are often used in 3D virtual worlds, such as Second Life (www.secondlife.com), but two-dimensional representations can also be used as profile pictures.

Some avatars can be programmed with speech, either as an audio clip or by converting text to speech. They can bring a multimodal dimension to text-based materials online, such as blogs, web pages and virtual learning environments, or be embedded into slideware presentations such as PowerPoint. Avatars can also be used as virtual characters in small movies to play out a role play or scenario.

How could I use them?

- Avatars can be used to create online animated movies to provide a creative way for learners to explore a particular topic or concept, or to demonstrate their understanding.
- Online courses can be supplemented with avatars to add another medium to the communication methods available, to stimulate engagement from a distance.
- Tutors can create speaking avatars to help learners understand what they have to do, presenting instructions and guidance verbally as well as in writing.
- Bring your blog to life with a speaking virtual character to give another method of communicating your information.
- Learners could be encouraged to design their own characters as profile images online, to represent themselves in social networking sites. This might be particularly useful for younger learners, where a photograph may be inappropriate.
- Using speaking avatars can be a motivating and engaging way to develop literacy and communication skills, as learners think about how best to get their messages across.

Where can I find them?

The Voki website allows users to easily and quickly create their own speaking avatars, for use in presentations, on blogs, or in profiles.

Click: www.voki.com

Xtranormal allows students to create online animated movies with 3D virtual characters from text. Debates, dialogues and scenarios can be created for the characters to play out, providing a creative and engaging way for learners to create a story or narrative.

Click: www.xtranormal.com

Anything I need to consider?

The creation of avatars will require access to computers and the internet. Microphones can also be used, although many take advantage of text-to-speech capabilities. Sometimes words need to be spelled phonetically to get the required pronunciation.

When playing back a virtual character with audio during a presentation, internet access will also be required in order to access the file.

Give it a go!

- Go to the Voki website and start to create your own avatar. Explore the different designs and accessories to personalize your character.
- Consider the different ways you can add speech to your avatar. Type in some text and press the preview button to hear them come to life! Check the pronunciation and spell phonetically if required.
- Save your avatar and explore the ways you can use the URL links and embed code to include in your blog.

What are others doing?

I use the Xtranormal movie with my pupils to explore parables and the effects of the Holy Spirit. They use the software to create a short story to express how their characters might be feeling, their emotions and their views.

It's a great way to get them all creatively engaged in the topic. Sometimes we use the best movies at open evenings and parent's evenings to demonstrate how they are using technology in their subject learning.

Claire – religious studies and citizenship teacher, secondary school

Find out more

Led by design collective 'body>data>space', Robots + Avatars is an innovative project exploring how young people will work and play with new representational forms of themselves and others in virtual and physical life in the next 10–15 years.

Click: www.robotsandavatars.net/education

22 Word clouds

What are they?

Simply, word clouds provide a visual representation of the most frequently used words on a blog or web page, or in a document or assignment. By entering text or a URL into the word cloud generator, a visual image is created which represents the frequency of the most popular terms in larger, bolder text.

Word clouds can provide a very quick indication of the key positioning and main themes of large documents. The visual representations can also be artistic and attractive in their own right. A variety of different shapes and designs can be chosen.

How could I use them?

- Learners can be encouraged to create a word cloud from their coursework evidence to explore the main themes which arise and whether these are aligned to the assessment criteria.
- Learners can also use word clouds as a starting point for critical discussions – for example, by analysing the key themes of political reports and documents, or the emphasis of news reports in different newspapers.
- Language and literacy skills can be developed as key terms are explored and defined, especially for speakers of English as their second or other language, or those with specific language needs.
- Word cloud images can be used to illustrate web sites and blogs to provide a visual representation of its content and style.

Where can I get them?

Tagxedo

Tagxedo produces word clouds in a variety of shapes, fonts, styles and colours to allow users to customize their design.

Click: www.tagxedo.com

WordSift

As well as producing a basic word cloud, WordSift has a number of other features which promote literacy development. Words can be ordered from most common to rare in alphabetical order. A visual thesaurus and dictionary function can help to decode words in context within the test, to develop a deeper understanding of their use and meaning.

Click: www.wordsift.com

Anything I need to consider?

Most word cloud software will only accept a maximum number of characters to be copied and pasted. Others will allow documents to be uploaded, for an increased number of words.

It is worth experimenting with different generators to ensure the output meets your needs.

Give it a go!

- Go to www.wordle.net
- Click on create and paste in some text from a handy document or report.
- Click 'go' to see the results! You can change the design by clicking on the randomize button to find one that suits your needs.

What are others doing?

I sometimes use WordSift in my higher level English for Speakers of Other Languages (ESOL) classes. Students are able to copy and paste text into the website to identify the most common words.

We can practise pronunciation as a group by sharing on the interactive whiteboard. The dictionary feature can also be a useful tool to work on vocabulary. I really like the fact I can order the words into the least common, so we can tackle a more challenging and unusual word.

Gail – ESOL and literacy tutor, adult and community learning

23 Comic strips

What are they?

A range of free, and user-friendly, websites now provide tutors and learners with the opportunity to create their own comic strips. This creative way to express knowledge and understanding can be used in the classroom, in computer suites, or as a directed learner activity.

Even those tutors lacking confidence with ICT can learn the basics in a few minutes, or even better – get the learners to demonstrate the technology!

How could I use them?

- Tutors can create their own comic creations to add originality to their slideware presentations or blogs.
- Learners can create their own strips to demonstrate their understanding of a particular topic, developing their creative expression.
- Literacy can be developed through digital storytelling as learners design their storyboards, create characters, and express emotions and language.

Where can I get them?

Both Bitstrips and ToonDoo provide a user-friendly interface to design and develop online comic strips, avatars and characters. Copy the screen to capture an image for use in coursework or on blogs.
Click: www.bitstrips.com/create/comic
Click: www.toondoo.com

Anything I need to consider?

Some of the overall functionality of free sites may be restricted and it is always advisable to let learners know if there are certain functions that they will not be able to use for their unique creations.

What are others doing?

I encourage my students to create a comic strip as a discussion point for the next lesson. They are able to use the famous characters available in Bitstrips to model some of the political satire comics found in many of the national papers to reflect a particular perspective on a policy decision or the latest U-turn.

Students complete their comics for homework on a rotation basis and they really look forward to seeing the next person's creative efforts. At the end of the term I award a prize for the most original creation.

Paul – politics lecturer, sixth form college

24 Digital posters

What are they?

Digital posters or graphics blogs (known as 'glogs') allow users to incorporate multimedia elements to design an appealing visual resource. Text, images, audio and video can be creatively combined to produce an interactive resource for engagement and exploration.

Posters can be shared, embedded or downloaded and used as product evidence or as interactive teaching tools.

How could I use them?

- Tutors can create their own glogs with multimedia features to act as stand-alone teacher resources for learners to interact with. As glogs are hosted online, learners can access at anytime to work through the information and activities included.
- Digital posters can be created by learners to demonstrate understanding of a particular topic or subject, developing their creativity and design skills. Learners can consider which online media is appropriate and free to use, developing their online digital wisdom and responsible internet use.
- Learners can work together to develop a collaborative piece – for example, putting together some assessment evidence for a piece of coursework. Available online, teachers can assess remotely and provide feedback quickly.
- Displayed via an interactive whiteboard, digital posters can be used at events, open days and parents' evening to present interactive information or a record of learner work.

Where can I get them?

Glogster provides an interface for the creation of digital posters. A free tutor account is also available for creating private glogs that can be shared with learners but not the wider world.

Click: www.glogster.com

Anything I need to consider?

With over seven million users worldwide, many different posters are created by many different users. As such, the content of some public glogs may not always be appropriate for younger learners and vulnerable adults.

The use of education accounts (www.edu.glogster.com) and codes allow for the more managed use of glogs in an education setting, where necessary. Learners can be sent a unique code to access only those glogs tutors create.

Learners should be aware of copyright restrictions when using online digital media.

Give it a go!

- Access the Glogster webpage and sign up for a free account or a free single tutor account.
- Click on 'Create new glog' and away you go. Experiment with adding text and images. Use the range of library images and backgrounds that Glogster provides.
- Make your poster interesting and attractive and try and add some multimedia content.
- Save and publish your poster to get the URL link. This can be shared with learners or colleagues for review and interaction.

What are others doing?

Learners often find it easier to express their understanding by producing creative evidence rather than writing assignments and essays. For one of the assignment tasks, my BTEC learners are asked to create a digital poster describing different promotional techniques and methods.

They use a range of images, including digital photographs of promotional methods they have taken themselves, and others from the Web. They can bring their posters to life with real examples which helps to contextualize and apply their work.

They also need to explain the difference between techniques and methods. The format of the digital poster allows some to type text explanations, while others prefer to record an audio clip to add to their images.

We can print a copy of the poster and I add an observation record as evidence of their multimedia content for their assessment files. This provides evidence of their knowledge and understanding.

Rani – lecturer in travel and tourism, further education college

25 VoiceThread

What is it?

The value of collaboration and discussion in classrooms and seminars is undeniably useful for the learning process, but it can be difficult to exploit this teaching tool in online courses or where students are unable to collaborate online at the same time.

VoiceThread provides a user-friendly online tool for capturing learners' online collaborative narrative asynchronously, in response to a visual stimulus or presentation.

Learners can participate remotely as a part of a working group or whole class, to express their thoughts and opinions. Users can revisit the threads to explore the new voices added or responses to the comments they have made.

Comments can be voiced through audio and video clip recordings or by typing text. Multiple comments can be made at each stage of a presentation or in response to a question from the tutor.

How could I use it?

- VoiceThread is often used to promote collaborative dialogue for learners participating in an online course at different times. Critiques, reflections, debates and presentations are all possible uses for this online software.
- Rather than coming together for an online webinar at a specific time, learners can view the presentation, document or image in VoiceThread and make their contribution. They can engage with comments from the tutor and other learners, consider, reflect and share.
- As comments are made asynchronously, learners have time to consider their responses, prepare and rehearse, and this may encourage less confident learners to make a valuable contribution more than in a real-time environment, which is more pressurized.
- Learners can be encouraged to start their own VoiceThread topics, with other group members required to critique the information presented as part of a formative assessment activity.
- Learners digital literacies and communication skills can be developed by listening to comments and making appropriate and pertinent responses through a variety of different mediums.

Where can I find it?

VoiceThreads can be created via the website. An app is also available for some mobile device platforms.

VoiceThreads can be shared by sending users the URL location or by embedding into a webpage or blog.

Click: www.voicethread.com

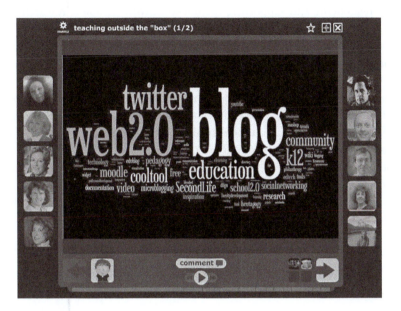

Anything I need to consider?

Users will need a webcam or microphone to add video or audio voices to a thread. Many of these are now built into laptops and mobile devices but may need to be configured for use with desktop computers.

Consider the content of VoiceThreads available in the public domain. Ensure that learners are commenting responsibly and not sharing personal data.

Give it a go!

- Access the VoiceThread website or download the app to your smartphone or tablet computer.
- Explore some of the existing VoiceThread examples to get a feel for what this is about and how it can be used.
- Create an account and create your first VoiceThread by uploading a few images or a small slideware presentation.
- Try and add some of your own comments to start with. Try adding text, an audio clip and a brief video clip.
- Name and save your VoiceThread and explore the options for sharing, embedding and inviting others to comment.

What are others doing?

I run an online course for trainee tutors. In one of the sessions we discuss the need and format for academic referencing and supporting written work with reputable research. Trainees only come together in online webinars every few months, so it was great to find a piece of software that could extend the online dialogue further in between the live sessions.

Following the group webinar, I uploaded a condensed version of my presentation, which featured some questions we had initially discussed together online. I encouraged trainees to revisit the information and these questions and to post their own responses having had more time to reflect.

As trainees are also working at different times, the VoiceThread format allows them to access and contribute to the discussion at a time which suits them. They like being able to watch and listen to their peers and then respond to the developing dialogue.

It was also really useful for me, as I had a record of their contributions and could remotely assess levels of understanding and engagement.

Lucy – teacher trainer, work-based learning

PART THREE
Conclusion

Chapter 2   Applying technologies in practice

In this chapter we present the experiences and voices of two beginning practitioners and their use of technologies.

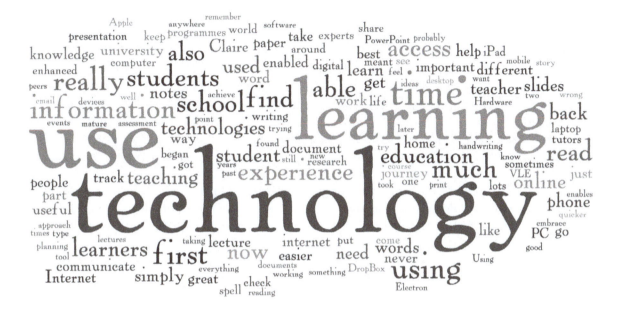

By the end of this chapter, you will have considered:

- how learners perceive technology and its use in their learning journey
- the tools that learners use to reduce barriers and facilitate learning
- examples of how learners would like practitioners to embrace technology in their approach to teaching, learning and assessment.

The Learner Voice

Claire is a mature student nurse who returned to education after a break. In her story, Claire describes the prominent feature of different technologies throughout her learning journey and the impact this has had on her progress and achievement.

Claire reflects on and evaluates how technology has enhanced her learning and offers some advice for practitioners considering harnessing the benefits in their own approaches to teaching, learning and assessment.

Pat is a newly qualified secondary teacher of design and technology, having just finished his teacher training postgraduate certificate. Pat reflects on how technology has enabled him to overcome some of the barriers he faced when learning with dyslexia.

Claire's story

My use of technology within my learning began at an early age. I suffer from very poor eyesight, which was not recognized before I began school. While other pre-school children were watching television, I was reading. Far from being a time in my life where I feel I missed out, this actually meant that I began school with the advantage of being able to read and write as I had an Acorn Electron at home – my first computer. I may not have been able to tell you my favourite cartoon show, but I could read, decipher, and act upon texts.

Moving through school (now with glasses, and a BBC Micro Model B at home) I was able to use the technology at school and get the best from it. I began my school life in 1989 at a time when technology-enhanced learning simply wasn't an important part of a child's education. I have distinct memories of being called out of a class, aged 8, to reboot the school's BBC Micro, which had stopped working, by a teacher who didn't know to press and hold 'Ctrl' and 'break'. To children now in classrooms with interactive whiteboards and high-speed internet access, this must seem like a time of the dinosaurs!

The Amiga was probably where the learning really started; the ease with which programs could be copied from one 3.5" floppy disc to another meant it was possible to own hundreds of programs. It really wasn't all serious though. My dad labelled all 12 disks of Monkey Island 2 from I to XII and presumably used this to teach my sister and I Roman numerals.

At home I had my first personal computer and my first dial-up internet connection in 1997. This did nothing short of revolutionizing my learning. A school report from my year 8 (aged 12–13) geography teacher stated: 'Claire's research skills are at a standard I would expect to see from a university student.' That comment specifically referred to a project where the class was asked to survey people about where they took holidays, and why. I did not simply phone relatives, but sent an email to members of a mailing list group my parents were members of through egroups.com (now part of Yahoo! Groups). I got hundreds of replies, which I was able to input into a database on Microsoft Works to collate and analyse the results. Even before the internet became the font of all knowledge it is now, there were programs such as MS Encarta (encyclopaedia software) which meant information could be more rapidly found than by using the 36 volumes of Encyclopaedia Britannica that still sit on my shelves.

My post-compulsory education continued to be supported by technology at a time when its use in school settings was growing. I was able to use the internet not just to gather information, but also to communicate with experts. An A level archaeology project resulted in me building working relationships with experts in that field.

In 2003, I moved out and went to university. My mum gave me bed linen, towels and crockery; my dad gave me a laptop and LAN cables of varying lengths (so I could access the internet from as far away from my desk as my bed). I used my first student loan payment to buy a Dell Pocket PC, a palmtop device to take lecture notes with; it could then be synced to my laptop which meant I wouldn't have to type them up. A digital camera soon followed, as did a mobile phone with wireless access (which I never used because it was prohibitively expensive to access the internet using the phone).

My first attempt at university was not a success. I left after one year and joined the rat race, working for an insurance company where technology was not used for learning but for business. The digital skills I had previously learned enabled me to progress in the company.

In 2010 I returned to university to study for a Diploma in Higher Education in Adult Nursing, and it is here that the integration between my learning and technology has really come into its own.

Shortly before starting university I bought a netbook, which I picked for its portability and because it worked well in conjunction with my home desktop PC. I was never one hundred per cent happy with the netbook as it was painfully slow. It genuinely took me back to watching the screen as I waited for the Acorn Electron to load Pac-Man from cassette.

I had been using an Apple iPhone for a while before returning to study and found the way it enabled me to access anything, anywhere, simply amazing. This led me to purchase a first generation Apple iPad to use for taking lecture notes, in much the same way the Pocket PC had been used over a decade earlier. This experience started my love affair with all things Apple, and in 2011 I bought a 21" iMac laptop, which brings my journey through technology (hardware) up to date.

Hardware, however, is only part of the story. Hardware is, in essence, a mere facility with which to access, create, view, amend, absorb and learn. It is, in its most basic, dissected form, lumps of metal, plastic and glass that act as windows to a whole universe of knowledge and experience. Hardware is a conduit by which information can be received and shared. To me, personally, it is very much two-way traffic.

I am Claire, 27, a mature student nurse. For me, technology is an essential part of my life. I find it so helpful and struggle to see how I would live the life I have now without it. It's useful in that everything can be synced, saving time, effort, and carrying a huge amount of 'stuff' around with me. It's helpful because it enhances my learning; it gives me access to everything – anywhere and anytime.

As a learner I feel technology is as important an aspect of education as any other. It is as vital as printed books, journals, lectures, workshops and, indeed, tutors.

The technology I use enables me to access information anywhere. The internet means I literally have an entire world's worth of knowledge at my fingertips 24/7. Online libraries and journal databases mean I can access professional texts, email, blogs and YouTube clips. Facebook and other social networks mean I can communicate with peers, academics and professionals at a time that suits me. Applications like Quora and Twitter mean I can engage in conversation with experts as well as peers. The internet is not simply an encyclopaedia of information; it's a tool to communicate and discuss information.

Software such as word-processing and desktop publishing programs enable me to communicate my learning – to collate, analyse and critique the information I find. Yes, it can be frustrating to use such a wide variety of technologies to simply type, print and hand in a typed paper document, but ultimately it enables me to publish my work, which in turn enables me to achieve grades and meet my learning goals.

Technology has enabled me to embrace areas of learning outside those required to simply pass my course. It has enabled me to participate in events such as BarCamps or 'unconferences'. These are user-generated conferences where the content is provided by the participants. BarCamps are events where the attendees run talks and workshops and any subject can be covered. You can go to a practical demonstration of virtual reality technology, followed by a debate on the use of IT in schools, and finish up with a talk on cocktail mixing!

I have also been able to participate in Hack Days where computer programmers, and those who (like me) do not know how to code, mix, exchange ideas and solve problems. These are just two examples of technology-enhanced events which, although not specifically aimed at my studies directly, have enhanced my learning experience by providing me with a broader knowledge gained from others.

Being a mature student I have experience in a professional workplace, but this took years to achieve, and many students have not come to education through this route. Many have progressed directly through school and further education to higher education. At the end of this journey they face being out there in the workplace with what could potentially be a very narrow view of the world. The use of collaborative online technologies has put me at the heart of a wide network of experts, tutors, peers and other students.

I have enrolled in online classes through Coursera (www.coursera.org). These free massive, open online courses (MOOCs) are a really interesting opportunity to supplement my learning and expand it in fields not already covered by my course. I also interact with people from around the world on their own learning journeys too!

In the classroom my use of technology is a vitally important part of my learning experience. I also attend my classes equipped with my iPhone and iPad to capture and record information, to communicate, and to collaborate.

I use Daily Notes, an app for the iPad, for taking notes in lectures. The user interface is simple and easy to use. It can also email notes in portable document format (PDF), which I can use when writing up my essays at a later date. This saves me so much time and keeps me organized.

I find Dropbox (www.dropbox.com) a really incredibly useful tool. When I make a note of something in a workshop or lecture on my phone, I can save the document to my Dropbox account. This instantly syncs with all my other devices, so I can add some further research to it in the library after the lecture on my iPad. When I get home, I can work on the document further using my desktop PC.

Weeks later, I can revisit it when discussing with a friend over coffee. I don't need to remember to take a memory stick or to back it up. All my documents go with me wherever I am through my mobile devices. Dropbox is the embodiment of everything I love about technology, enabling the 'anytime, anyplace' philosophy that I have adopted with my learning.

I also use an e-reader which I find really useful for reading journal articles, which can be viewed as PDFs and e-books. It saves me having to print off and carry around lots of different bits of paper, and I can find lots of small gaps of time to get in some reading.

There can be frustration too of course. The different formats of technology can cause issues with compatibility at times. Documents available through the VLE are not always compatible with the devices I am using. And sometimes the procedures that you also have to follow in education can be frustrating – for example, having to print and physically submit my work by driving miles through traffic when it would be much quicker and easier for me to submit it online.

As well as the use of technology for research and assignment work, its use in direct teaching is important too, and I have seen lots of changes. Being sat in a lecture hall can often be described as Death by PowerPoint, and I have seen lots of different uses by my tutors – some good, some not so good. PowerPoint does have a place, but its place is not 72 slides, with five paragraphs on each, and a tutor who reads the slides word for word.

Nothing makes my heart sink faster and deeper than taking a seat and seeing a lecturer desperately trying to get their presentation to load and seeing the sheer bulk of what is to come. If I could write a rule book for tutors I'd probably start with this:

- Don't tell a student that they don't need to take notes because it will all be on the VLE later and then read the slides verbatim – and, especially, please don't then forget to put the slides on the VLE.
- Don't use the standard slideware templates. If your students have six lectures in a day they really might struggle to take in what you're saying at 4 p.m. when they've spent the last six hours looking at six people who all used what looks to be the same presentation.
- Do check your hyperlinks. Embedding YouTube clips or links to external sources into a presentation is great, but only if it works. Please do a quick run through first.
- You know your stuff and we don't. Yet. You've got an hour, you've got 80 slides; please don't rush. We're here to learn and we want to learn. We genuinely want to hear what you have to say and it's really disappointing when you say, 'I've only got an hour, so I'll have to skip most of this.' Please

adapt your presentation to the time you have available, otherwise we think we've missed out on the slides we didn't get to see!

- Be different! Try Prezi instead of PowerPoint. It will give you a headache the first time you use it, but the first time you see someone else using it you do sit up in your seat. It's a change, and sometimes a change is good. Be that forward-thinking tutor, teacher or lecturer that people leave the classroom of and say, 'I never expected that.'

- If a student has their phone out, then don't assume they're playing games. If you put a diagram up and asked me to copy it I wouldn't even dream of getting a pen out; I'd probably copy something wrong, learn it wrong, and quote it wrong in an exam. I'll take a picture of it. I won't take notes on paper; I'll type them up. When I'm using my mobile device I promise I'm not planning my Friday night out!

- Embrace new ideas. The world is changing all the time, and technology seemingly changes faster than anything else. I'm only 27, and I've gone from my basic Acorn Electron to all this. Where will I be in another 27 years? Where will I be in 27 months in terms of what technology I use and want other people to use?

- The biggest, most important message I could give anyone is to embrace what comes your way. Give it a shot. If it doesn't work then put it down to experience. The very best teachers I've had are the ones who say to their students, 'What do you use?', 'Why did you do it that way?' The best educators are the ones who are still students, or at the very least still try to think like their students.

Pat's story

The use of technology has changed dramatically in the years since I left school, and this has been a great thing. I use my laptop and smartphone almost all the time to sort out my planning for lessons and to keep in touch with what is happening around the world.

The internet has become the best library I have every used. You can quickly find what you are looking for, but need to be careful not to lose yourself in it and lose track.

I use software programs to check on my spellings and grammar, which has made getting to grips with dyslexia so much easier. Spelling and grammar checks in my word-processing program have been such a great tool of modern technology for me, as you can check these and correct them with such ease.

Even words that I could never spell before I can attempt to spell and use now, using the technology to keep me on track. In the past I would sometimes have changed these to ensure I could spell them, losing the thought trail that I had. But now I have improved so much with this that I am not afraid any more to express myself in words.

Having software read my own written words back to me has given me so much help to ensure that I am writing what I am trying to say and not losing track. I have lost my thought trail so many times before when trying to spell a challenging word, often without even noticing!

The worry of not being able to read my own handwriting is now a thing of the past. I just start writing my thoughts into a Word document to record, and then edit them after the computer has read them back to me. In the past I would have done this on paper, but my handwriting would become harder and harder to read the more I was writing, as my thoughts would have developed quicker than I could get them onto paper.

Reading through loads of books to find quotes or references has been made easier with the use of technology. Using 'quick search' to find a starting point to read from and research has been a great experience which I have shared with others.

As an educator you can develop your teaching with written words and extend these with links to the internet and share them with students. Students can then develop these ideas again further and share them back to you – all through the power of online technologies. Your feedback will be quicker and easier to share and no one will ever say 'I could not read your handwriting.'

You can explain so much more with pictures and words. Sometimes one good image can say more than thousands of words. Combining the two, and doing this more and more, will make it easier to do. It helps to differentiate your teaching to meet the needs of individuals – some learn better from very visual resources.

I have found in my first week as a newly qualified teacher that keeping a diary of what is happening each day is very useful, as you have so much information given to you, which is hard to keep track of at times. Using online technologies has really helped with this process. I can go back and find what I need to at any time using my online calendar and notepad. I can add and review information quickly using my smartphone. I don't need to try and remember my diary everywhere I go, but I always remember my phone!

Planning is a big task you come across as a new teacher, and using technology to help you can be really valuable. I use some of the free applications to help with my planning, to keep my documents together and to keep track of all those useful websites. It can sometimes be difficult to learn new technologies, but don't be afraid to ask if you don't understand something. Often your students will be able to point you in the right direction!

Reflection point

We invite you to reflect on Claire and Pat's stories and to consider your own learners and their experience of technology – from a personal perspective, but also their experience of their tutor's use of technology.

- Do you feel that their advice is appropriate to you and your practice?
- Would you ask your learners for their views on your own use of technology in your approach to teaching?
- How might your learners benefit from an increased use of technology tools where it has the power to enhance learning and their outcomes?
- Are your learners digitally wise and how does the learning journey you share together prepare them for a digital, knowledge age?

Moving forward

However you decide to use technology in your approach to teaching, learning and assessment, we hope that pedagogy comes before the technology. Using multimodal and multimedia approaches can help to engage and motivate our learners to achieve their learning goals, demonstrate their creativity, and prepare for their digital futures.

The need to stay informed and connected is paramount and technology can help to facilitate and strengthen these rich social networks.

Appendix 1: IRIS reflection template

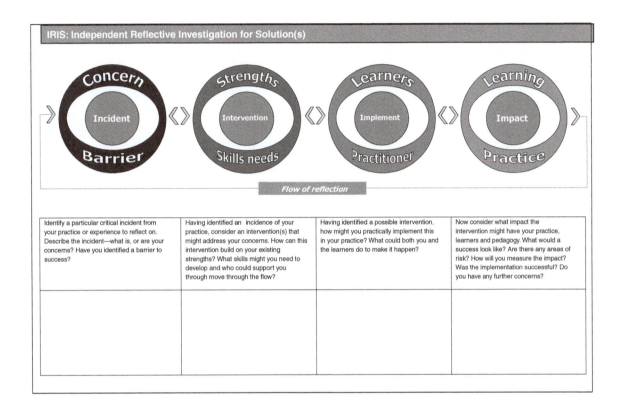

IRIS: Independent Reflective Investigation for Solution(s)

Concern — Incident — Barrier
Strengths — Intervention — Skills needs
Learners — Implement — Practitioner
Learning — Impact — Practice

Flow of reflection

Identify a particular critical incident from your practice or experience to reflect on. Describe the incident—what is, or are your concerns? Have you identified a barrier to success?	Having identified an incidence of your practice, consider an intervention(s) that might address your concerns. How can this intervention build on your existing strengths? What skills might you need to develop and who could support you through move through the flow?	Having identified a possible intervention, how might you practically implement this in your practice? What could both you and the learners do to make it happen?	Now consider what impact the intervention might have your practice, learners and pedagogy. What would a success look like? Are there any areas of risk? How will you measure the impact? Was the implementation successful? Do you have any further concerns?

Appendix 2: Pecha Kucha storyboard template

1	2	3	4	5
6	7	8	9	10
11	12	13	14	15
16	17	18	19	20

Appendix 3: Mobile device student loan agreement template

Responsible E-mail, Internet and ICT Use Please complete, sign and return to the Administrator	
Student:	Form:
Student's Agreement I have read and understand the school 'E-mail and Internet Use Good Practice - Rules for ICT Users' document. I will use the mobile device in a responsible way and obey these rules at all times. I understand that if I break any of these rules, I may have access to email, internet and ICT removed.	
Signed:	Date:
Parent / Carer's Consent for Internet Access I have read and understood the school 'E-mail and Internet Use Good Practice - Rules for ICT Users' document and give permission for my son / daughter to access the Internet using the mobile device. I understand that the school will take all reasonable precautions to ensure students cannot access inappropriate materials. I understand that the school cannot be held responsible for the nature or content of materials accessed through the Internet. I agree that the school is not liable for any damages arising from use of the Internet facilities. I understand that if my child breaks any of the rules regarding the safe access of all ICT facilities then they may have access to them removed.	
Signed:	Date:
Please print name:	
Signed:	Date:

Bibliography

Anderson, P. (2007) *What is Web 2.0? Ideas, Technologies and Implications for Education*. Bristol: JISC. Available at www.jisc.ac.uk/media/documents/techwatch/tsw0701b.pdf [Accessed March 2012].

Anderson, T. and Whitelock, D. (2004) The Educational Semantic Web: Visioning and Practicing the Future of Education, *Journal of Interactive Media in Education*, 1: 1–15. Available at www-jime.open.ac.uk/article/2004-1/181 [Accessed October 2012].

Armstrong, K. (2009) From I.A. Richards to Web 3.0: Preparing Our Students for Tomorrow's World, *World Academy of Science, Engineering and Technology*, 58: 954–61.

Attewell, J., Savill-Smith, C., Douch, R. and Parker, G. (2010) *Modernising Education and Training: Mobilising Technology for Learning*. London: LSN.

Barton, D. (1994) *Literacy: An Introduction to the Ecology of Written Language*. Oxford: Blackwell.

Barton, D. and Hamilton, M. (1998) *Local Literacies: Reading and Writing in One Community*. London: Routledge.

Barton, D., Ivanič, R., Appleby, Y., Hodge, R. and Tusting, K. (2007) *Literacy, Lives and Learning*. London: Routledge.

Beetham, H. and Oliver, M. (2010) The Changing Practices of Knowledge and Learning, in R. Sharpe, H. Beetham and S. de Freitas (eds) *Rethinking Learning for a Digital Age*, 155–69. London: RoutledgeFalmer.

Bennett, S., Maton, K. and Kervin, L. (2008) The 'digital natives' debate: a critical review of the evidence, *British Journal of Educational Technology*, 39(5): 775–86.

Bonk, C. (2007) *USA Today Leads to Tomorrow: Teachers as online concierges and can Facebook pioneer save face?* The blog of Dr Curt Bonk. Available at http://travelinedman.blogspot.co.uk/2007/10/usa-today-leads-to-tomorrow-teachers-as.html [Accessed May 2012].

Brookfield, S. (1995) *Becoming a Critically Reflective Teacher*. San Francisco: Jossey-Bass.

Brown, P., Lauder, H. and Ashton, D. (2008) *Education, Globalisation and the Knowledge Economy*. London: Teaching and Learning Research Programme (TLRP). Available at www.tlrp.org/pub/documents/globalisationcomm.pdf [Accessed December 2011].

Bullen, M., Morgan, T. and Qayyum, A. (2011) Digital Learners in Higher Education: Generation is Not the Issue, *Canadian Journal of Learning and Technology*, 37(1). Available at www.cjlt.ca/index.php/cjlt/article/view/550/298 [Accessed January 2012].

Campbell, J. and Finegan, W. (2011) Dawn of the Social Cyborg, *Training Magazine*, 10 July. Minnesota: Lakewood Media Group. Available at www.trainingmag.com/article/dawn-social-cyborg [Accessed July 2011].

Carmigniani, J., Furht, B., Anisetti, M., Ceravolo, P., Damiani, E. and Ivkovic, M. (2010) Augmented reality technologies, systems and applications, *Multimedia Tools and Applications*, 51(1): 341–77.

Carstens, A. and Beck, J. (2005) Get ready for the gamer generation, *TechTrends*, 49(3): 22–6.

Caruso, J. and Kvavik, R. (2005) ECAR study of Students and Information Technology, 2005: Convenience, Connection, Control, and Learning. Boulder, Colorado: EDUCAUSE. Available at http://net.educause.edu/ir/library/pdf/EKF/ekf0506.pdf [Accessed February 2010].

Casey, H., Cara, O., Eldred, J., Grief, S., Hodge, R., Ivanic, R., Jupp, T., Lopez, D. and McNeil, B. (2006) *'You Wouldn't Expect a Maths Teacher to Teach Plastering...' Embedding Literacy, Language and Numeracy in Post-16 Vocational Programmes – The Impact on Learning and Achievement*. London: National Research and Development Centre for adult literacy and numeracy.

Conole, G., de Laat, M., Dillon, T. and Darby, T. (2006) *JISC LXP Student Experiences of Technologies: Final Report*, JISC report. Available at www.jisc.ac.uk/whatwedo/programmes/elearning_pedagogy/elp_learneroutcomes [Accessed March 2011].

Dalgarno, B. and Lee, M. (2010) What are the learning affordances of 3-D virtual environments?, *British Journal of Educational Technology*, 41(1): 10–32.

Dede, C. (2005) Planning for Neomillennial Learning Styles: Shifts in students' learning style will prompt a shift to active construction of knowledge through mediated immersion, *EDUCAUSE Quarterly*, 28(1): 7–12.

Dewey, J. (1933) *How We Think: A Restatement of the Relation of Reflective Thinking to the Educative Process*. Boston: D. C. Heath.

Duckworth, V. (2008) *Getting Better Worksheets*, Adult Literacy Resources. Warrington: Gatehouse Books.

Duckworth, V. (2009) *On the Job: Car Mechanic Tutor*, 1st edn, Into Work 14–19 series. Warrington: Gatehouse Books.

Duckworth, V. and Tummons, J. (2010) *Contemporary Issues in Lifelong Learning*. Maidenhead: Open University Press/McGraw-Hill Education.

e-Learning Foundation (2012) *e-Learning Foundation – About us*. Available at www.e-learningfoundation.com/about-us1 [Accessed May 2012].

Ellis, M. and Anderson, P. (2011) Learning to teach in second life: a novice adventure in virtual reality, *Journal of Instructional Pedagogies*, 6: 1–10.

Ferguson, R. (2011) Meaningful learning and creativity in virtual worlds, *Thinking Skills and Creativity*, 6(3): 169–78.

Gee, J. P. (1996) *Social Linguistics and Literacies: Ideology in Discourses*, 2nd edn. London: Taylor & Francis.

Gee, J. P. (2000) Teenagers in new times: A new literacy studies perspective, *Journal of Adolescent & Adult Literacy*, 43(5): 412–20.

Gibbs, G. (1988) *Learning by Doing: A Guide to Teaching and Learning Methods*. Oxford: Further Educational Unit, Oxford Polytechnic.

Goodfellow, R. and Lea, M. (2007) *Challenging E-learning in the University*. Maidenhead: Open University Press.

Green, M. (2011) Better, Smarter, Faster: Web 3.0 and the Future of Learning, *Development and Learning in Organizations*, 25(6): 70–2.

Guo, R., Dobson, T. and Petrina, S. (2008) Digital natives, digital immigrants: an analysis of age and ICT competency in teacher education, *Journal of Educational Computing Research*, 98(3): 235–54.

Harasim, L. (2010) *Learning Theory and Online Technologies*. Oxford: RoutledgeFalmer.

Head, A. J. and Eisenberg, M. B. (2010) *Truth Be Told: How College Students Evaluate and Use Information in the Digital Age*, Project Information Literacy Progress Report. Seattle: The Information School, University of Washington. Available at http://projectinfolit.org/pdfs/PIL_Fall2010_Survey_FullReport1.pdf [Accessed February 2012].

Higgins, S., Kokotsaki, D. and Coe, R. (2011) *Pupil Premium Toolkit: Summary for Schools Spending the Pupil Premium*. Available at http://educationendowmentfoundation.org.uk/uploads/pdf/Pupil_Premium_Toolkit_%2820.12.11%29.pdf [Accessed May 2012].

Hillier, Y. (2002) *Reflective Teaching in Further and Adult Education*. London: Continuum.

Holley, D. and Oliver, M. (2011) Negotiating the Digital Divide: Narratives from the Have and the Have-Nots, in R. Land and S. Bayne (eds) *Digital Difference: Perspectives on Online Learning*, 101–14. Rotterdam: Sense Publishers.

Holloway, S. and Valentine, G. (2003) *Cyberkids: Children in the Information Age*. London: RoutledgeFalmer.

Holmes, B. and Gardner, J. (2006) *e-Learning: Concepts and Practice*. London: Sage.

Howe, N. and Strauss, W. (2000) *Millennials Rising: The Next Generations*. New York: Vintage Books.

Hughes, A. (2009) *Higher Education in a Web 2.0 World*, JISC report. Available at www.jisc.ac.uk/publications/generalpublications/2009/heweb2.aspx#downloads [Accessed December 2010].

Ivanic (2008) *Harnessing Everyday Literacies for Student Learning at College*. London: Teaching and Learning Research Programme. Available at www.tlrp.org/pub/documents/IvanicRB50final.pdf [Accessed December 2011].

JISC (2008) *Exploring Tangible Benefits of e-Learning*, JISC report. Available at www.jiscinfonet.ac.uk/publications/publications/info/tangible-benefits-publication [Accessed January 2012].

JISC (2012) *Learning in a Digital Age: Extending Higher Education Opportunities for Lifelong Learning*, JISC report. Available at www.jisc.ac.uk/media/documents/publications/programme/2012/JISCLearninginaDigitalAge.pdf [Accessed 20 June 2012].

Johnson, L., Adams, S. and Cummings, M. (2012a) *NMC Horizon Report: 2012 Higher Education Edition*. Texas: The New Media Consortium. Available at http://net.educause.edu/ir/library/pdf/HR2012.pdf [Accessed April 2012].

Johnson, L., Adams, S. and Cummings, M. (2012b) *NMC Horizon Report: 2012 K-12 Education Edition*. Texas: The New Media Consortium. Available at www.nmc.org/publications/2012-horizon-report-k12 [Accessed June 2012].

Klein Dytham Architecture (2011) *Pecha Kucha: What?* Available at www.klein-dytham.com/pechakucha/what [Accessed May 2009].

Kolb, D. (1984) *Experiential Learning as the Science of Learning and Development*. New Jersey: Prentice Hall.

Lenhart, A., Rainie, L. and Lewis, O. (2001) *Teenage Life Online: The Rise of the Instant-Message Generation and the Internet's Impact on Friendship and Family Relationships*. Washington: Pew Internet and American Life Project.

Lohnes, S. and Kinzer, C. (2007) Questioning assumptions about students' expectations for technology in college classrooms, *Innovate*, 3(5). Available at www.innovateonline.info/pdf/vol3_issue5/Questioning_Assumptions_About_Students'_Expectations_for_Technology_in_College_Classrooms.pdf [Accessed October 2012].

Margaryan, A., Littlejohn, A. and Vojt, G. (2011) Are digital natives a myth or reality? University students' use of digital technologies, *Computers & Education*, 56: 429–40.

McEneaney, J. E. (2011) Digital Literacies: Web 3.0, Litbots, and TPWSGWTAU, *Journal of Adolescent and Adult Literacy*, 54(5): 376–8. Available at https://files.oakland.edu/users/mceneane/web/research/web_and_litbots.pdf [Accessed March 2012].

McNamara, M. (2007) *Getting Better*. Warrington: Gatehouse Books.

Milgram, P. and Kishino, F. (1994) A Taxonomy of Mixed Reality Visual Displays, *IEICE Transactions on Information Systems*, E77-D(12): 1321–9.

Moon, J. (1999) *Reflection in Learning and Professional Development: Theory and Practice*. London: Kogan Page.

Morris, R. (2011) Web 3.0: Implications for Online Learning, *TechTrends*, 55(1): 42–6.

Noss, R. et al. (2012) *System Upgrade: Realising the Vision for UK Education*. Technology Enhanced Learning Research Programme. London: London Knowledge Lab.

Oblinger, D. (2003) Boomers, Gen-Xers and Millenials: Understanding the 'New Students', *EDUCAUSE Review*, 38(4). Available at http://net.educause.edu/ir/library/pdf/erm0342.pdf [Accessed April 2010].

Oblinger, D. (2004) The Next Generation of Educational Engagement, *Journal of Interactive Media in Education*. Available at www-jime.open.ac.uk/jime/article/view/2004-8-oblinger [Accessed October 2012].

Ofcom (2011) *Communications Market Report: UK*, UK Communications Regulator Research Report. London: Ofcom. Available at http://stakeholders.ofcom.org.uk/binaries/research/cmr/cmr11/UK_CMR_2011_FINAL.pdf [Accessed April 2012].

Ohler, J. (2008) The Semantic Web in Education, *EDUCAUSE Quarterly*, 31(4): 7–9. Available at http://net.educause.edu/ir/library/pdf/EQM0840.pdf [Accessed March 2012].

Ohler, J. (2010) The Power and Peril of Web 3.0, *Learning & Leading*, 37(7): 14–21.

O'Reilly, T. (2005) *What is Web 2.0: Design Patterns and Business Models for the Next Generation of Software*. Available at www.oreillynet.com/pub/a/oreilly/tim/news/2005/09/30/what-is-web-20.html?page=1 [Accessed March 2012].

Palfrey, J. and Gasser, U. (2008) *Born Digital: Understanding the First Generation of Digital Natives*. New York: Basic Books.

Pang, L. (2009) A survey of Web 2.0 Technologies for Classroom Learning, *The International Journal of Learning*, 16(9): 743–59.

Parry, D. (2011) Mobile Perspectives: On Teaching Mobile Literacy, *EDUCAUSE Review*, 46(2). Available at www.educause.edu/EDUCAUSE+Review/EDUCAUSEReviewMagazineVolume46/iMobilePerspectivesOnteachingi/226160 [Accessed April 2012].

Pedro, F. (2006) *The New Millennium Learners: Challenging our Views on ICT and Learning*. OECD Centre for Educational Research and Innovation (CERI). Available at www.oecd.org/dataoecd/1/1/38358359.pdf [Accessed August 2011].

Prensky, M. (2001) Digital Natives, Digital Immigrants, *On the Horizon*, 9(5). Available at www.marcprensky.com [Accessed June 2011].

Prensky, M. (2009) H. Sapiens Digital: From Digital Immigrants and Digital Natives to Digital Wisdom, *Innovate*, 5(3). Available at www.innovateonline.info/index.php?view=article&id=705 [Accessed February 2011].

Prensky, M. (2011) Is the Digital Native a Myth? No, *Learning & Leading with Technology*, 39(3): 6–7.

Rhodes, C., Stokes, M. and Hampton, G. (2004) *A Practical Guide to Mentoring, Coaching and Peer-networking*, London: RoutledgeFalmer.

Schön, D. A. (1983) *The Reflective Practitioner: How Professionals Think in Action*. New York: Basic Books.

Seely Brown, J. (2009) *Learning in a Digital Age*. Available at http://net.educause.edu/ir/library/pdf/ffpiu015.pdf [Accessed March 2012].

Selwyn, N. (2008) *Education 2.0? Designing the Web for Teaching and Learning*, A TLRP-TEL Programme commentary. London: TLRP-TEL. Available at www.tlrp.org/pub/documents/TELcomm.pdf [Accessed March 2012].

Sharpe, R., Beetham, H., De Freitas, S. and Conole, G. (2010) An introduction to rethinking learning for a digital age, in R. Sharpe and H. Beetham (eds) *Rethinking Learning for a Digital Age*, 1–12. London: RoutledgeFalmer.

Siemens, G. (2005) Connectivism: A learning theory for a digital age, *International Journal of Instructional Technology and Distance Learning*, 2(1): 3–10.

Siemens, G. (2008) *Learning and Knowing in Networks: Changing Roles for Educators and Designers*. Presented to ITFORUM for discussion. Available at http://it.coe.uga.edu/itforum/Paper105/Siemens.pdf [Accessed April 2012].

Street, B. (1984) *Literacy in Theory and Practice*. Cambridge: Cambridge University Press.

Tamim, R., Bernard, R., Borokhovski, B., Abrami, P. and Schmid, R. (2011) What Forty Years of Research Says About the Impact of Technology on Learning: A Second-Order Meta-Analysis and Validation Study, *Review of Education Research*, 79(3): 1243–89.

Tapscott, D. (1998) *Growing up Digital: The Rise of the Net Generation*. New York: McGraw-Hill.

Tapscott, D. (2008) *Grown Up Digital: How the Net Generation is Changing Your World*. Toronto: McGraw-Hill.

Thomas, M. (2011) *Deconstructing Digital Natives: Young People, Technology and the New Literacies*. London and New York: Routledge.

Traxler, J. and Wishart, J. (2011) *Making Mobile Learning Work: Case Studies of Practice*. Bristol: ESCalate, The Higher Education Academy. Available at http://core.kmi.open.ac.uk/download/pdf/309713/3 [Accessed April 2012].

Tummons, J. (2007) *Becoming a Professional Tutor in the Lifelong Learning Sector*. London: Learning Matters.

Veen, W. (2003) A new force for change: Homo Zappiens, *The Learning Citizen*, (7): 5–7.

Waycott, J., Bennett, S., Kennedy, G., Dalgarno, B. and Gray, K. (2009) Digital Divides? Student and staff perceptions of information and communication technologies, *Computers & Education*, 54(4): 1202–11.

Yuen, S., Yaoyuneyong, G. and Johnson, E. (2011) Augmented reality: An overview and five directions for AR in education, *Journal of Educational Technology Development and Exchange*, 4(1): 119–40.

Zhou, F., Duh, H. B. L. and Billinghurst, M. (2008) Trends in Augmented Reality Tracking, Interaction and Display: A Review of Ten Years of ISMAR, *IEEE International Symposium on Mixed and Augmented Reality* (IEEE/ACM ISMAR), 193–202.

Index